When Yo
Quitting Teaching, Read
This Book

When You Feel Like Quitting Teaching, Read This Book offers hope to educators, helping you remember the joy of the profession through the power of great teaching and learning. The book provides inspiring stories along with clear strategies to make teaching more meaningful and manageable. Common teaching issues, such as increasing student engagement and motivation, improving structure, maximizing prep and assessment time, reconsidering student–teacher interactions, and establishing positive teacher collaborations and support are given a fresh, relevant approach. Appropriate for teachers of any subject or grade level, the book will leave you with inspiration as well as practical takeaways to help you stay reinvigorated on your professional journey.

Bill Manchester (@bmanchester_edu) is a 17-year (and counting) veteran teacher whose career has been marked by creativity and high student engagement. He also manages the website *ADifferentEduSite.com* and hosts the podcast *A Different EduPodcast.*

When You Feel Like Quitting Teaching, Read This Book

Inspiration and Strategies for Long-Term Success

Bill Manchester

Routledge
Taylor & Francis Group

NEW YORK AND LONDON

Cover image: © Getty Images

First published 2022
by Routledge
605 Third Avenue, New York, NY 10158

and by Routledge
4 Park Square, Milton Park, Abingdon, Oxon, OX14 4RN

Routledge is an imprint of the Taylor & Francis Group, an informa business

Library of Congress Cataloging-in-Publication Data
Names: Manchester, Bill, author.
Title: When you feel like quitting teaching, read this book : inspiration and strategies for long-term success / Bill Manchester.
Description: New York, NY : Routledge, 2022. | Series: Routledge eye on education | Identifiers: LCCN 2022000865 (print) | LCCN 2022000866 (ebook) | ISBN 9781032169996 (hardback) | ISBN 9781032157603 (paperback) | ISBN 9781003251330 (ebook) Subjects: LCSH: Teachers--Job stress. | Teachers--Job satisfaction. | Teaching--Psychological aspects. | Classroom management. | Burn out (Psychology)
Classification: LCC LB2840.2 .M24 2022 (print) | LCC LB2840.2 (ebook) | DDC 370.15--dc23/eng/20220124
LC record available at https://lccn.loc.gov/2022000865
LC ebook record available at https://lccn.loc.gov/2022000866

ISBN: 978-1-032-16999-6 (hbk)
ISBN: 978-1-032-15760-3 (pbk)
ISBN: 978-1-003-25133-0 (ebk)

DOI: 10.4324/9781003251330

Typeset in Palatino
by SPi Technologies India Pvt Ltd (Straive)

Contents

Acknowledgements

I am the product,
    not the sum,
    of the teachers that have gone before me.

A sum is simply additive, whereas a product builds upon itself. Each of the learning experiences I have had has built upon the last one in ways that are factors greater than they would have been on their own. I have received an incredible progression of teaching experiences that have made me the teacher and learner I am today. I was happy to be able to reference over 25 former teachers and colleagues in the book, but there are many others that I have learned from and rely on. I hope to write much more and continue to recognize and honor all the great teaching and learning that constantly inspires and sustains me. To all the staff and administration at Maysville Middle/High School, Westhills Elementary, the Muskingum University Music Department, and Bexley City Schools, thank you for your support and sustenance.

Next a special thank you to Lauren Davis, my publisher. Her teaching background continues in her editing work, being able to see where a student is heading, not just where they are at currently. She approached this project in that way and I am grateful that I was not judged simply on my initial drafts.

Thank you to my parents and my sisters. Not only were my parents my earliest examples of great teachers, but they have continued to support me emotionally and practically in the teaching profession. My older sister was another one of my early teachers, showing me how to always be kind and love others deeply. My younger sister was one of my first students and our hour-long trumpet lessons, which were often filled with as much laughter as music, convinced me that teaching was something I could be happy doing for a long time.

My wife and daughters are my biggest support. This book would not have been possible without the love, energy, and tireless work of my wife Jeanette, supporting behind the scenes as she has all through our relationship. She supported my writing by joining my middle school newspaper staff when we were 13 and her love and support has only grown over the years. My daughter Oliviya has also been an incredible support, letting me talk her ear off about education ideas and being my assistant teacher for a hundred or so summer math, reading, and music workshops. I will treasure the late nights sitting at the kitchen counter, getting feedback from Oliviya on my manuscript while I helped her with her calculus homework. And thank you to my two-year-old daughter Lilli, who supported this endeavor by accompanying me on a number of trips to local coffee shops across Columbus and "encouraging" me to take lots of breaks with her at the nearby playgrounds.

Meet the Author

Bill Manchester is a full-time teacher in Bexley, Ohio. From guiding the tremendous growth in kindergartners to harnessing the overwhelming energy of pre-teen summer math students to directing the high level of technicality in a university music ensemble, Bill has gotten hooked on the power of great teaching and learning which has kept him in the classroom for 17 years and counting. Bill lives with his wife Jeanette and their two daughters, Oliviya and Lilliona. They enjoy playing music together, traveling, photography, various caffeinated beverages, and Peppa Pig. You can connect with Bill on twitter (@bmanchester_edu), his website *ADifferentEduSite.org*, and the podcast he hosts, *A Different EduPodcast*.

Introduction

When You Feel Like Quitting Teaching – An Allegory

To begin, I am borrowing some pedagogy from black pastors in the US. One of the lessons I have learned is the use of an "anchor text" in the sermon. A pastor might begin the message with "our text for today comes from…" and then reference a well-known biblical passage, often a story, that the congregation would have some familiarity with. After a brief summary, the pastor will bring out particular insights and interpretations about the passage. The use of the anchor text means that the congregation is with him from the beginning. The audience is already anticipating where the sermon is heading. If the message is good, the congregants will also continue to think about it any time the passage is brought up again.

In this tradition, my text today comes from the book of Aesop's Fables, the story of the Fox and the Grapes. A fox comes upon a bunch of grapes high on a branch. After increasingly drastic but unsuccessful leaps and jumps, the fox exclaims, "why am I wearing myself out for a bunch of sour grapes?"

There are so many times when this seems to describe exactly what teachers are feeling. Running from meeting to meeting that seem to exist only for the purpose of documenting that we are documenting. Jumping and leaping to meet standards solely as defined on an endless series of high-stakes standardized tests.

DOI: 10.4324/9781003251330-1

Wearing ourselves out to plan and prepare detailed, intricate lessons that fall flat, often for reasons that seem outside of our control.

The emergency pandemic teaching that many teachers experienced over the past year intensified this exhaustion. Daily, posts on social media revealed high-profile teacher leaders wondering if they would be able to continue. And even if we can, is it worth it?

Like the fox, I have found myself tired and exhausted, thinking about the promise of great teaching and learning that is not always realized and exclaiming, "why am I wearing myself out for a bunch of sour grapes?" This book is about that moment and what happens next.

The fable of the Fox and the Grapes shows us two important things about this moment. First, the grapes are ripe and delicious and worth running and jumping for.

During the fall of the pandemic year, I organized a virtual workshop with a local regional orchestra. They performed Richard Maltz's suite on Aesop's Fables, which included the story of the Fox and the Grapes. During the Zoom conference call and in the music classes preceding it, students were running and jumping with the clarinet flourishes and snare drum exclamations that Maltz used to make the fox's antics come alive. Students at home jostled in and out of the camera fields on the Zoom screen, enthusiastically moving to the music. In class we spread out all over the stage running and jumping with the musical cues and exclamations.

After all of the running and jumping, the students and I talked about the story. For kindergartners and first graders particularly, I first had to convince them that the grapes were, in fact, not sour. In the beginning of the story, the narrator gushes about the fullness and ripeness of these grapes. The timpani is heard, posing as the grapes, ready to burst with sweet juice. Following the best practices in literacy instruction, we used the textual evidence to show us that what the fox said was incorrect and that the grapes were indeed delicious and definitely worth running and jumping for.

It is not that simple when it comes to evaluating what we do as teachers and how students respond. How do we know that we are not just wearing ourselves out for sour grapes? The first purpose of this book is to provide evidence of the sweetness of the grapes. Educating children is really a wonderful, magical experience that is worth running, jumping, and striving for. Hopefully, the stories and examples in the book will inspire and confirm this for you; moreover, the goal is for these stories to be a starting point to think about the stories and examples from your own teaching and learning that renew your belief and commitment to the power and magic of education.

The second lesson from the fable is what the fox does next. After the textual evidence convinced my students that the grapes were not sour and the fox really wanted them, I asked what moral he might learn from the story. Our working definition of a moral was a lesson about what to do or what not to do. Students suggested that the fox build a ladder, jump on a trampoline, and all sorts of other means to get the grapes.

Note, this is not about working harder or longer. Thinking about that moment is not about mustering the courage at 11 p.m. to put on another pot of coffee and work through the night to produce the world's greatest lesson. There was a unanimous consensus among the kindergartners and first graders that the moral of the story was not that the fox should just run and jump more. It was clearly physically impossible for him to reach the grapes. Even with their imaginative ideas about helpful bears, giraffe friends, and helicopters, none of them suggested that the fox simply continue to work harder at what was not working.

Teaching has always been demanding and exhausting. I was talking about this book to my brother-in-law's mom and she said, I've felt like quitting teaching, but here I am in year twenty-five still going strong. For others, the increasing demands of teaching have proven to be too much. And there is a third group that didn't quit teaching, but they are not going strong. As the years went by and particularly during emergency pandemic teaching, it felt like the branches were too far away and perhaps it was all sour grapes anyway. It became easy to run a little less and jump a little lower. What's the point if we're only chasing sour grapes?

For those of us still running and jumping, leaping toward those beautiful grapes, this is a time to recommit and reaffirm all the things we love about teaching and learning and clarify and intensify the tools we can use to move past the obstacles that get in our way of that ideal.

It is at this point in a sermon that a pastor might ask the congregation for a response. He might ask them to come forward to the altar or kneel down in the pews or walk to the microphone to testify. I just ask you to turn the page.

1

When You Feel Like Quitting

Practical Advice

On May 4, 2021, EdWeek released the results of a poll showing that 54% of teachers felt it 'likely" or "somewhat likely" that they would be leaving the teaching profession in the next two years. When teachers were asked how they thought they would have answered the question in the fall of 2019 before emergency pandemic teaching, 34% answered "likely" or "somewhat likely." Based on these data, in a given year, one out of every three teachers feels like quitting. After emergency pandemic teaching, every other teacher felt like quitting.

Fortunately, many of the teachers that feel like quitting don't. The exit rates for teaching have remained around 8%, although researchers often point out that there are wide variances according to the school situations. There is also speculation that the effects of emergency pandemic teaching on teaching morale and retention have yet to be fully expressed in the number of teachers leaving the profession. Even if rates double, many teachers feel like quitting teaching, but don't.

Feeling like quitting, but not quitting also has a cost. Teachers experience tremendous stress and fatigue living with the cognitive dissonance of doing a job that is very different than what they want it to be. This is expressed in many ways. For some teachers it's "I need to create healthy boundaries for when I am going to work outside of the school day because it is all too

DOI: 10.4324/9781003251330-2

overwhelming." For some, "I can't stand to even think about school for a second longer than I have to." "I am really looking forward to taking a break over Thanksgiving" and "I need to call off tomorrow because I just can't take another day." For me it was "I need to wait until I have eaten a good meal and rested a few hours before I can even begin to think about tomorrow's lessons" and eventually "I am spending money to work with a professional counselor to be able to handle the stress I am feeling about teaching."

Whether we prefer it or not, our physical condition powerfully affects our mental condition. How we feel about anything is always related to how our bodies are feeling. When we are tired, hungry, or ill, the non-well-being of our physical bodies will translate into a non-well-being of our mental selves.

In my faith tradition, there are many stories of people not giving up. When things get tough, whether through the protagonist's own choices or through the actions of others, the ancient texts give instructions on how to go on.

In one of these stories, a prophet Elijah is worn out from "doing God's work." He travels to a deserted, desert spot and announces to God that he is done. He would prefer to die rather than go on. Rather than perform some miraculous sign, God sends angels with food and then the prophet takes a nap. The idea of "self-care" is nothing new. It was ingrained in these sacred texts from thousands of years ago.

When you feel like quitting, when teaching feels overwhelming, attending to these physical needs – diet, sleep, and overall health – is the first key to being able to make long-term decisions based on these feelings. Take a nap, eat a good meal, and do what you can to feel good physically before unpacking strong feelings about quitting teaching.

When teachers enter the profession, they tend to give answers like the following to why they decided to become a teacher:

◆ I want to make a difference
◆ I like kids
◆ I love the subject that I will be teaching
◆ I want to make learning fun

In 2016, the Learning Policy Institute released a report detailing reasons that teachers left the profession. Their list of reasons teachers were leaving included:

♦ salaries and other compensation;
♦ preparation and costs to entry;
♦ hiring and personnel management;
♦ induction and support for new teachers
♦ working conditions

(Podolsky, A., Kini, T., Bishop, J., &
Darling-Hammond, L. (2016). Solving the Teacher
Shortage: How to Attract and Retain Excellent Educators.
Palo Alto, CA: Learning Policy Institute.)

The two lists are distinct. This means that generally when teachers enter the profession because "I want to make a difference," they are not leaving because all of the sudden they no longer want to make a difference. They are leaving because another factor, as listed above, is getting in the way of their primary motivation.

This is important because it means that for many teachers their feelings of quitting teaching are not about thinking they made a mistake – I thought I wanted to make a difference, but I actually don't. The feelings about wanting to quit teaching are tied to specific problems and obstacles, many of which can be overcome.

While salaries, teacher preparation, and hiring practices are beyond the scope of this book, support for teachers (both new and old) and working conditions are factors that teachers can often have a direct impact on. The teaching profession is based on the idea that students can learn, grow, and change. Teachers should be the best at this. There are ways that teachers can learn, grow, and change to affect and influence the conditions they are working in and the support that they are receiving.

This book is a way of organizing that information and providing hope that things can get better.

The next chapter, Chapter 2, outlines the three necessary components of teaching and learning: content, engagement, and environment. Teachers can use this framework to confidently plan effective lessons and troubleshoot less-than-effective ones.

Chapter 3 provides additional research-based tools for affecting change in your classroom that can be applied very quickly.

Chapter 4 deals with classroom management, specifically how to structure your class in a way that students can grow in their learning.

A part of "working conditions" that many teachers find particularly challenging is the amount of prep work needed for effective lessons. Chapter 5 provides hope and tools to make planning manageable and meaningful.

Many teachers report a negative working environment due to the pressures of standardized testing. Chapter 6 tells how and when to ignore these tests, and, moreover, how to put the tests into the appropriate context.

Although the effect has specifically been studied in new teachers, feelings of isolation pull teachers of all levels out of the teaching profession. Chapter 7 shows how collaborative working relationships keep teachers teaching.

The number one reason that teachers continue to teach is the power of great teaching and learning. Chapter 8 celebrates this power as well as showing how to recognize the signs of great teaching and learning and help students define and celebrate great teaching and learning.

In the story referenced earlier about the prophet Elijah, after a month and a half of letting Elijah work out the physical parts of his trials, God finally addresses Elijah's situation directly. One of Elijah's major complaints was that he was all alone in the good work he was trying to do and no one could understand what he was going through. In a still, small voice, God tells Elijah this is not true. He is not alone in the good work he is trying to do.

You are not alone in the good work you are trying to do. It is vital to realize that other teachers have felt this way before and that, more importantly, other teachers have felt this way before and then stopped feeling this way before.

The sign on the door was my name and under it said EMR class- educable mentally r*******.

This is Martha. She started teaching special education at an elementary school in 1973. "I think I had 12 students.

And ranging in grades one to five. I didn't have good diagnostic records for these children. Basically, I had their IQ scores there because that's what got them into the class."

Particularly at this time, IQ scores were seen as a stable measure of a student's intelligence. Once a student received a certain IQ score, it was expected that it would remain stable throughout their life. That meant that once a student entered the special education class, they would stay there throughout their academic career. But an interesting thing started to happen in Martha's classroom.

Students tested out of my classroom and if you know anything about the EMR label it was based on IQ. So generally IQ shouldn't change. They shouldn't be testing out of my classroom, but they did. They did.

In addition to calling into question the reliability of IQ testing, this showed the incredible teaching and learning that was happening in Martha's classroom. But it didn't start out that way.

"I will be honest, it was very chaotic." Martha was in a class with twelve students in an age range corresponding to 2nd to 5th grade. While some students might have been able to work on similar objectives, Martha was essentially planning twelve individual lessons for five and half hours every day in all subject areas.

There was no record or paperwork saying okay, this is the reading level of this student. This is the reading level of this student. This is where this student is in math. I had nothing, absolutely nothing. Every night I would come home and I was planning day to day because I never knew for sure what was going to work, how the children would react to it, and plus I was trying to figure out where they were to even begin to teach them.

This need for intense planning takes a toll on teachers and for Martha the added behavioral challenges multiplied the stress. "The children, would I mean literally... run out of the room... if they didn't like what I was doing, they just ran out of the room.

By Thanksgiving I was just done… I was not enjoying my time. I loved the kids but I just felt like I wasn't doing anything for them."

By winter break, Martha's feelings about quitting teaching had reached an action point. "This is the point where I said I'm done. I'm not ever teaching again. I told my husband I said I'm not a quitter. I will finish the year. Somehow I will get through the year. But when this year is over I'll be looking for a different occupation. I'm not doing this ever again." Notice the frustration was so intense, Martha was not just looking for a new teaching assignment, but a whole new occupation. Even after devoting four years of college to a career in education, she was ready to give it all up just thinking about the possibility that it might never get better. "I was done. I just felt like I can't. I can't do this. I would not. I didn't feel that I could risk taking another job in any form of teaching because I just felt like I don't ever want to be in this place again. It was just so frustrating and I felt so inadequate and I felt bad for the kids. I just felt like I am not doing the job here."

In the weeks leading up to winter break, Martha had started to implement a behavior modification system. "I started collecting popsicle sticks and these were plastic popsicle sticks. They came in all different colors back then. And I called my friends, everybody I knew, I said, save your popsicle sticks for me and I managed to collect quite a large number." These popsicle sticks became currency in Martha's classroom. It was a clear way for her to communicate to the students the types of behaviors the class would require. "What I would do sometimes is if there were one or two who were really acting out, rather than take away from them, I rewarded everyone else and commented on what they were doing. I didn't say anything about what the children who weren't doing what they were supposed to be doing." The students were able to exchange the popsicle sticks at her "store" for a tangible expression of the desired behavior – small trinkets she had bought and brought in to school. "Catching them being good. That's what I was doing."

Momentum began to build. Martha was able to assess student levels and provide appropriate instruction due to the popsicle stick behavior modification system. Students were learning exactly what behavior was needed and were able to positively engage in the content Martha was providing. As Martha mentioned, the whole time she loved these kids deeply and as she demonstrated that through her teaching, the students felt loved and valued. This momentum building was slow and largely imperceptible for a long time. Martha expected to return to school in January with one foot out the door looking for a new career and life direction. Instead…

"When we went back, I really found that I had missed those kids. They were like a family. We really had bonded and even the kids bonded with each other because I really tried to help them develop relationships with each other and to be kind and it was really a family." Martha had seen how her hard work and love for those kids had paid off. "It was like a different classroom and I had a better hold on how I could individualize and keep the other children busy while I was working with one."

With an extrinsic reward system like Martha was using, educators might wonder if it can continue to be effective. Will increasingly large rewards be needed to maintain the desired behavior? If the extrinsic rewards are taken away, will that erase the students' motivation for appropriate behavior? As the momentum continued to build in Martha's classroom, there was indeed a shift in the rewards that students were working for. "By the end of the year I loved what I was doing and I will say the next year I never used behavior modification with the popsicle sticks again. The next year… I wondered, … am I going to have some of these kids say, well, where's our popsicle sticks? But they didn't." The rewards that the students were now getting from great learning, caring relationships from their peers, and a teacher that loved them were worth far more than the small trinkets the students had been trading their popsicle sticks for.

> They like knowing what's expected of them and they were really responding. I was finally starting to feel like I was making progress and they were learning. I mean, it was very rewarding. I loved it. I loved those kids. By the end of the year, I thought I'll never quit doing this.

Martha Manchester didn't stop teaching. She continued to teach at the elementary school for the next five years. Because she didn't quit teaching, her experience taught the staff and community that her students had so much more potential than the label that they had been assigned. Later she became the founder, director, and lead teacher of Rainbow Nursery School, a play-based, discovery-style pre-school.

Everywhere Martha went, she was a teacher. In her faith community, for the past fifty years she has taught children, youth, and adults, often from her own living room. She was constantly involved with the local schools, voluntarily taking on teaching roles and initiatives that would be typically reserved for paid faculty as well as filling in difficult to find long-term subbing positions outside of her original training. For many years she led pre-school literacy programs at the local library. Understanding that learning is more than academics, for years she ran a free after-school program that included homework help and meals. In her current role as a member of the state school board of Ohio, she continues to work to provide every student all of the possible opportunities to reach their potential. She is also my mom.

(Martha's story is an excerpt from the episode "#DidntQuitTeaching: Martha, the Intervention Specialist" from *A Different EduPodcast*, written and hosted by Bill Manchester, first released in January 2021.)

How Do I Use This Tomorrow?

At the end of each chapter, there is a list of suggested reflection questions/activities. The ideas in this text will have the most significant impact on your teaching practice if you are able to specifically apply them. By spending a few minutes answering the questions/completing the reflection activities, you can develop specific steps to implement tomorrow to make these ideas a part of your teaching practice.

1. What things make you want to keep teaching? How can you increase these benefits? (Check out Chapters 7 and 8.)

2. What things make you want to stop teaching? What of these can you control? Do you think you can make enough change in the areas that you can control to continue teaching? Are you willing to try? If you identify strongly with any of the subjects listed specifically, skip to that chapter first to hear about other teachers who have struggled with the same issue and how they have been able to keep going.

How Do We Learn This Together?

Being able to discuss, digest, augment, and personalize information is a great way to be able to learn and apply concepts. If you have an established group of collaborative colleagues, I encourage to work through these discussion questions in a group. For those looking to establish or expand their collaboration networks, each chapter includes a hashtag suggestion for posting ideas, stories, questions, and support on social media networks. You can also search these hashtags to see how other educators are applying these ideas.

#DidntQuitTeaching. Post about a time when teaching got tough, but you were able to push through. These could range from funny or awkward moments to significant obstacles that forced you to decide whether you could believe in the power of great teaching and learning.

Martha Manchester did not come into her elementary special education classroom with all of the skills, knowledge, or experience needed to be successful immediately. She was able to learn and grow in the components of teaching necessary for her students to be successful. While each specific teaching situation requires specific teaching, there are components of teaching that are universal. Understanding these components is a first step in establishing confidence as a teacher in any situation. We'll start digging into these in the next chapter.

2

The Learning Triangle

Content, Engagement, and Structure

Figure 2.1 depicts the relationship between teaching and learning. The teacher transmits content to the student. Then the student is given an opportunity to confirm the transmission of this content. If the content is confirmed, the teacher continues with additional content. If the transmission of content is not confirmed, the teacher clarifies, explains, breaks down, and re-teaches the information. Then the cycle repeats.

There are three different components the teacher is managing to facilitate this learning.

Outside of the specific **content** being presented (represented by the shapes), there is a quality to a classroom that makes students feel safe and energized to participate in their learning. This **structure** (represented by the building), combined with opportunities for students to respond to the material and create a feedback loop with the teacher (**engagement** – represented by the arrows), facilitates great learning and teaching.

When there is more than one student, the teacher is managing these three components for each student, including how the student-to-student interactions affect content, engagement, and structure (Figure 2.2).

Figure 2.3 is teaching and learning online. In online teaching, the content and engagement are mediated by the technology being used by the students and teachers. The teacher may not be

DOI: 10.4324/9781003251330-3

FIGURE 2.1 Learning between a Teacher and Student.

FIGURE 2.2 Learning between a Teacher and Class.

able to present the content in the same way. Students also may be limited in the opportunities they have to engage with the content. The teacher also has far less control and influence over the structure of the environment in which the students are learning.

Figure 2.4 details teaching and learning in a hybrid classroom in which some students are learning online and some students are face to face. Note the complexity of feedback cycles and directions. Also note how the teacher has control over various parts of the learning structure for some students, but not for others. Those students who are physically present have a different set of engagement opportunities than the online students.

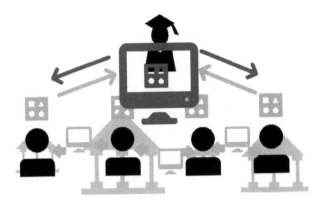

FIGURE 2.3 Online Learning.

FIGURE 2.4 Hybrid Learning.

There are limitations to the two-dimensional models shown in these figures. Classrooms should not center the teacher or one particular student. So imagine this diagram rotating. Now imagine that the rotation is sometimes occurring without provocation by the teacher and that, at other times, the teacher is carefully rotating it while participating in it, as if in a giant hamster ball.

When teaching feels overwhelming and particularly online and/or hybrid emergency pandemic teaching, these figures explain why. Teachers experience stress due to the plethora of interactions that they are trying to produce, manage, and manipulate in order to create the conditions necessary for great learning to occur.

The Learning Triangle

Fire professionals use the fire triangle to be able control and utilize fire. Knowing that a fire requires minimum amounts of fuel, oxygen, and heat, these components can be used in various combinations to achieve desired fire levels. The fire triangle for learning, by contrast, is content, engagement, and structure. Each of these components is necessary at a minimum level for learning and the components can be used in various combinations to achieve the desired learning levels.

During emergency pandemic teaching, engagement and structure changed drastically for most students. Some students struggled precisely because their teachers had been so good at engagement and/or structure in their in-person classrooms. Structure and engagement strategies are often based on real-time, in-person interactions that cannot be directly translated virtually.

During the online, emergency pandemic teaching, a parent in my district posted the following about her first-grade daughter's experience with emergency pandemic learning to Facebook:

> ... And then sometimes I just have to get work done so I let her crawl in my lap and hold her while I work and then she tells me that she loves writing when she's at school but hates it at home. And then she says...because after you finish writing at school you get to have a meeting with Mrs Young and so I usually hurry up and finish 'cause I really want to meet with her [crying face emoji] and then I fill up with tears cause this little girl just misses her teacher so much [heart emoji].

Thinking about teaching in the context of the learning triangle allows teachers to reflect on the full gestalt of the learning experience. Having a multi-faceted framework to use while planning and a diagnostic tool to evaluate lessons that are less successful gives teachers confidence and predictability in their ability to produce great teaching and learning. This lowers the stress and tension associated with wondering how a lesson is going to go or whether the preparation has been adequate.

Content

Content is generally the least adjustable part of the learning triangle. Content is often dictated by local, state, and even national standards. Beyond that, local districts and buildings are often looking for consistency, which often means even greater standardization of texts, programs, and approaches. In most classrooms, the content is not designed to be reflective and reflexive of what a specific group of students want to learn, but rather what they "need" to learn, as determined by local, state, and national education leaders.

However, teachers generally still maintain a large amount of control over the manner in which content is presented. Even if the content is very rigid, the perspective and approach to the content can make a significant difference in how the content is received by students and how easily they engage with the content.

Math standards are very specific. In the Grade 8 math standards in Ohio, students begin to informally create equations that fit given data. One way to approach this standard would be give students raw data without any meaning and have them attempt to draw graphs that fit the data and then approximate the equations.

Another approach would be to have students gather real-life data about correlations they notice, plot them into a spreadsheet and use the spreadsheet plug-ins that automatically create a variety of graphs to compare what kind of graphs would best fit the data they have inputted. After posting their results online, students would evaluate which types of equations were the best fit for their data and their classmates' data. Students are learning about how graphs fit real-life data and then lessons can be easily differentiated by adjusting the types of graphs students are producing with the software.

Deliberate selection and presentation of content makes it easier for students to engage.

Engagement

Engagement is defined by the opportunities that students are given to respond to the content and the feedback loop that is created as the teacher responds to students' responses. For the purposes of planning and evaluating lessons, it is useful to qualify this component as engagement *opportunities*. Whether the students actually take advantage of these opportunities is largely dependent on the students' connection to the content and the learning structure the teacher has established.

In order for the teacher to know that learning has taken place, there has to be a minimum level of engagement opportunity that the student participates in to demonstrate the learning. The minimum level of engagement opportunities needed is defined by the specificity of the learning objectives that are being taught. However, having the right amount of engagement opportunities and adjusting variables such as time between opportunities and depth of opportunities can make a significant difference in student engagement.

For example, when student participation levels in the engagement opportunities are low (both quantitatively and qualitatively), providing more shallow, easy engagement opportunities at the beginning and throughout the lesson will generally increase the quality and quantity of student participation.

Writing song/rap lyrics is a favorite unit of mine to teach. When I was working with middle-school students, I had a number of students that produced incredible fully formed pieces that not only fit the formal structures of song lyrics (rhyming, verse-chorus-bridge form, etc.), but were also full of emotion expressed through a variety of figurative language. It would often take very little instruction for them to begin working. Within a few class periods and without much feedback, these students would be writing incredible lyrics, producing loop-based backing tracks, recording vocals, and "releasing" the rap to wide acclaim on our online class learning management system.

Working with fourth graders, I quickly found that I needed to give them many more opportunities to engage with writing lyrics in very simple ways (fill in the blanks on a given theme, create raps on multiplication facts, etc.) before they were able to engage at a full-length original song level. Once the students had engagement opportunities at a lower level earlier in the lesson sequence, they were able to produce much more fully developed ideas at the end of the sequence.

Determining the type, rate, and level of engagement opportunities based on the content and environment gives the teacher the necessary information to know whether learning has taken place.

Structure

The structure of the class is created by the relationship between the teacher and the student and the students to each other. A positive, safe, energetic structure makes it easier for students to engage in any kind of content.

Young students love to sing into the microphone. As students get older, often an environment develops in which students feel like their singing will be critiqued harshly and they stop wanting to sing by themselves on the microphone. With these older students, particularly in middle school, a small change in the environment can suddenly make all the difference. Often one brave soloist performing at any level shows how the class will respond and how the teacher will be able to manage the responses. If the responses are positive and managed, the effect on student participation is immediate and significant. Soon there is a line and it is often the case that not everyone is able to get a turn before the class period is over. (This idea of small changes having a large effect has been studied by behavioral scientists and will be explored more in the next chapter.)

Great teaching and learning involves spending energy, taking risks, and knowing that growth, rather than perfection, is the goal of any learning opportunity. When this structure is established, students more quickly engage with content and produce great learning.

Classroom Management

Classroom management challenges can generally be seen as a deficit in one or more areas of the learning triangle. If the content is not of interest to students, they will tend to find other activities that are more interesting. If the content offers insufficient engagement opportunities with the content, students will seek out alternative engagement activities. If the appropriate structure has not been established, when learning requires risk taking, students will not take those risks.

Reflecting on and addressing possible deficits in the learning triangle is a first step in proactive and reactive classroom management. A well-planned lesson that sufficiently addresses each component of the learning triangle is the best way to address classroom management challenges. Specific and targeted strategies for managing behaviors in the classroom with content, engagement, and environment will be detailed in Chapter 4.

Use In Planning

The learning triangle can be used in planning to establish predictability and prepare for flexibility.

Content. What is the bridge between what students want to learn (or what you think they want to learn) and the stated objective for the lesson? What options/flexibility are there in the presentation and framing of this learning objective? Are there ways to anticipate student interest and be prepared for surprises? Are there opportunities to specifically gather student interest in the topic to build the lesson around?

Engagement. How quickly will students be able to interact with the content? How could a variety of engagement opportunities be available for students? How could technology be utilized to offer engagement opportunities? How reactive will the teacher be able to be to student responses?

Structure. How has the structure been established? Are there particularly emotionally/socially risky portions of the lesson that might need to be preceded by environment/relationship building activities? What relationship-building activities could be prepped as part of the lesson or ready as responsive teaching?

Use As a Diagnostic Tool

When a lesson does not go well, it can seem logical to abandon everything in the lesson and start again from scratch. Using the learning triangle as a diagnostic tool enables teachers to keep the best parts of the lesson and correct the components that need new direction.

This is also a way to diagnose lessons among teaching colleagues. When a lesson does not go well, there is often an emotional piece that causes a need for venting and expressing of emotions without problem solving. It is vital we allow each other this emotional space. Once a teacher is ready to problem solve, the learning triangle provides a strengths-based approach to move forward.

Content. Did you connect with the content? Is there anything you could do to make the content more exciting to yourself to teach? Did the content connect with the students? What is something in the lesson in which they were interested? Are there applications of this concept in students' lives that can be presented to connect with students?

Engagement. What engagement opportunities did students take advantage of? Could these opportunities be expanded? Were all activities required? Could more choice in engagement activities encourage more participation? Could less choice encourage more interaction between students working on the same thing? What additional engagement opportunities could be offered? What was the timing of the engagement opportunities? Could lower-level engagement opportunities be presented sooner? Or would students be more stimulated by moving to higher-level problems faster? Would more time before engagement opportunities allow for more instruction, thereby increasing student success?

Environment. What emotional and social risk taking is required in the lesson? If students were not taking risks, how could these risks be lowered? When students took risks and were vulnerable, were you able to maintain the desired classroom environment? If not, could engagement opportunities become more private and/or more optional? What relationship-building activities could be added to the lesson to reinforce the values of the classroom? Are there student leaders in the class that could be utilized strategically to reinforce the desired classroom environment?

As these questions are applied to a "failed" lesson, a small adjustment can make the difference between frustration and success. (A categorical list of these changes, many of which can be quickly applied to any lesson, will be provided in the next chapter.)

Leveraging the Learning Triangle

While teaching, including all areas of the triangle, is a combination of skills that are developed over time through practice and often research, many teachers are naturally strong in one or more areas of the triangle. This strength is often what inspires teachers to enter the profession to begin with. Certain teaching situations that lean heavily to one side of the triangle are often advantages at the beginning of a teacher's career, but they can turn into disadvantages when a different teaching situation requires more attention in another area of the triangle in which a teacher may not be as naturally gifted.

A minimum level must be met in each component, so teachers need to be ready to address all components of learning in vigorous ways. However, as teachers identify their strengths, they can learn to leverage them to make teaching more manageable.

Leveraging Content

In fourth grade at Waynesfield-Goshen elementary school, I was fortunate to be able to participate in a pull-out program with the Gifted Specialist Vicki Agnew. Vicki Agnew has an incredible gift for presenting and teaching content in trans-disciplinary, multi-optioned, genre/subject-defying ways.

I still remember our virtual race across the United States. We raced from Washington, DC to San Francisco, California. Each student carefully determined their route on paper maps detailing the highways of the United States. Miles were earned by diary entries, reports, and other research into the cities and regions we were passing through.

Geography content was taught and practiced as we carefully worked to find the best routes. Math content favored heavily as we added the mileage between markers on the map, subtracted the mileage from what we had earned, and estimated how much we might earn for the next leg of the journey. Math become more applied as we compared one route to another. A more direct route through rural areas might mean less miles, but also more difficult research. Language Arts skills were honed as we wrote reports and journal entries all about the research we had completed as we moved forward in the journey.

The engagement opportunities for this project carried a relatively high cost. Before internet resources, research meant rummaging through the class library or the class set of encyclopedias. Trips to the school library became a necessary last resort for hard to find content. Even with these relatively high costs, I was motivated by the way the content was presented to work as hard as I could. Any down time in class became research and writing time for me to continue on the race. I was working harder at all of the work at school that I was doing so that I might earn more free time to do this preferred work.

Leveraging content can mean that students are more likely to be willing to pay a high cost for engagement opportunities.

Leveraging Engagement

Engagement opportunities are often directly related to the content being presented, but engagement can also be leveraged in non-content-related ways. This can be especially helpful in situations in which there is little time to expand or modify content and limited opportunities to influence the classroom environment.

Substitute teaching is exactly this kind of situation. At one point in my middle-school teaching tenure, we had an incredible "guest teacher," Kim Rhodes. She was a retired teacher with a well-respected record of strong teaching in a neighboring district. While her years of experience certainly gave her clarity and wisdom as classroom situations arose, one of her tools particular to guest teaching was her word of the day. Whatever the subject, Kim would select a random word of the day (often of the SAT vocabulary-type). She would then have students digest the word and come up with ways to use it in context. Students enjoyed the challenge and the immediate interaction they received. Because students participated and received positive feedback right away, they were more likely to participate and engage throughout the rest of the period. When Kim was a guest teacher, her classes were consistently well-behaved and effective in achieving the objectives that the classroom teacher had left.

I saw a similar engagement technique used by another excellent guest teacher. When my wife was completing her master's degree in counseling, she was also a guest teacher in the elementary school where I taught. She routinely had students working to earn the reward of doing more work. She had some new, different work for the second-grade students that she put on the back table. Students could access this only when they had completed the assigned work from their teacher. Students worked hard to complete the assigned work just to be able to engage with the new, special work from the guest teacher.

Leveraging engagement means lowering the barriers to beginning and maintaining a feedback cycle. Once a feedback cycle has been initiated, a safe, trusting environment begins to develop which makes any content easier to learn.

Leveraging Structure

Structure is being leveraged when students are actively engaged in activities that might not make a lot of sense without the context of the classroom in which they are taking place.

Jonathan Juravich, an elementary art teacher and the 2018 Ohio Teacher of the Year, had his students decorating circles for a cardboard house. These multi-colored circles look interesting on the five-foot mini house Jonathan had assembled, but the pedagogical purpose might not be immediately apparent.

In his 2018 TedTalk "How Do You Teach Empathy?," Jonathan explained that this was part of a unit he had been teaching fourth graders on architecture. But the students didn't need to decorate a house with multi-colored circles to learn about architecture. The multi-colored dots were emulating the work of two famous artists that cover houses with polka dots. While re-creating the polka dot houses might have been a good way to learn about these artists, it was so much more than that.

Each dot represented a student response. A student response that Jonathan had engineered after he and his students discussed the destruction Hurricane Harvey had caused. Jonathan had created a space in his classroom where students felt safe and respected. This space also inspired them to want to create those spaces for other children, particularly in the midst of tragedy and need. Each dot was a student donating art supplies to students in Houston after the hurricane.

These houses were more than multi-colored dots on cardboard, they were a physical representation of the environment that Jonathan and his students learned in and believed in to the point of wanting to spread it to other students halfway across the country.

The emotional environment that Jonathan had created meant once he set up the content and engagement opportunities, his students were begging to be a part of the teaching and learning he was engineering.

On good days when teaching and learning is "natural" and full of joy, it is easy to see it as a gift or an art rather than a set of practical skills that can be developed and refined. When teaching gets hard, using the learning triangle can highlight the skills a teacher needs to develop and refine in order to make a lesson successful. Dissecting lessons into the various components often quickly reveals the changes that can be made to make the lesson successful.

How Do I Use This Tomorrow?

1. Which part of the learning triangle is strongest and most natural to you as a teacher? How have you or could you leverage that for increased student learning?
2. Which part of the learning triangle do you feel the most constrained in by building or district policies? Have you ever tried to push back on this constraint? Are there areas where you might be able to introduce more flexibility by talking to administrators/supervisors?
3. Are there any lessons/plans that you have had high hopes for, but feel far short of expectations? Using the questions earlier in the chapter (p. 22), consider whether you might be able to use the learning triangle as a diagnostic tool to be able to realize fully the potential of your plan.

How Do We Learn This Together?

#LearningTriangle. Give an example of how you saw engagement, structure, and content working together beautifully in a classroom, maybe yours or a colleague's.

In particularly difficult situations, it may not be clear what changes need to be made and/or it may seem like the changes needed are so significant that they are impossible to consider and implement. However, a small change may be the catalyst that creates a chain reaction in a lesson to move from failure to success. The social science research behind the phenomenon as well as specific examples that can be applied to most lessons will be discussed in the next chapter.

3

Little Things That Can Make a Big Difference

In their 2008 book, *Nudge: Improving Decisions About Health, Wealth, and Happiness*, Economics Nobel Prize winner Richard Thaler and Harvard law professor Cass Sunstein created specific vocabulary for affecting outcomes with small design changes. They describe trying to influence these changes as "nudges" and dub bosses, parents, teachers, and other influence leaders as "choice architects," with a unique ability to influence the choices students, children, employees, and citizens make in a way that will greatly affect outcomes.

With the amount of control teachers have over schedules, décor, lighting, eating, drinking, and even room temperature, "choice architect" is a fitting addition to a teacher's title. Great teachers have always considered many options to increase student learning. These nudges help students push through mental, emotional, and social blocks to learning. While nudges have been explored in a variety of educational contexts, this chapter specifically focuses on nudging to overcome the short-term mental, emotional, and social blocks that keep or delay students from participating and fully engaging in rewarding educational experiences.

One of the facets to Thaler and Sunstein's work on nudges is helping people manage short-term decisions to support long-term rewards. In much of their work, the scale of time between

DOI: 10.4324/9781003251330-4

short-term decisions and long-term rewards is years or even decades. When dealing with retirement accounts, the result of a nudge to start saving more may not be seen for thirty years or more.

In teaching, the use of a nudge can be much more immediately gratifying. The scale of time between overcoming a short-term block for a more long-term reward can be minutes.

This gratifying use of nudge was very clear in a music class I observed several years ago. In February 2012, President Obama invited an all-star cast to "educate" the country and the world on the beauty, resiliency, and power of the blues. As the president was beginning to exit the concert hall during the finale, blues legend Buddy Guy invited his star student to take on a more participatory role in the lesson. Buddy Guy wanted Obama to sing a chorus of the final number, "Sweet Home Chicago."

During a short interchange, Obama politely declines, smiling and mouthing the words, "not tonight." Blues master B.B. King nudges, "you can do it." In the recording for PBS, the camera operator catches Obama's "oh-man-I-don't-really-want-to-do-this-but-how-can-I-say-no-to-these-guys" face. He is the reluctant student, not sure he is ready to get in front of his peers and be vulnerable.

But the nudges push him forward. He takes a breath, puts on a brave face, and accepts the microphone with another smiling nudge from none other than Rolling Stones front man Mick Jagger. President Obama delivers an incredible vocal performance and the gigantic smile on his face after singing the final line leaves little doubt that he was very happy with his choice to actively participate in the lesson. In a few minutes, he has been nudged through his short-term block and received the long-term reward of a successful educational experience.

This educational experience seemed to have had an even longer-term reward. Years later when President Obama gave the eulogy at the funeral of Rev. Pinckney, killed in a shooting at a Charleston church, Obama confidently led the congregation in an a cappella rendition of "Amazing Grace." While his closest advisors, including his wife, had been skeptical of his plan to sing a solo that would no doubt reverberate across the world, he remained confident and self-assured, perhaps buoyed by the encouraging nudges he had received at the White House from the blues legends.

To be clear, I was not present for the "class" at the White House or at Rev. Pinckney's funeral to see Obama's enduring musical growth. (There is extensive footage online of both performances which are worth watching multiple times.) While I cannot claim to be intimately familiar with Obama's musical education, the progression from reluctance to overwhelming joy, helped by a nudge, and the enduring effect is one that I and many educators find very familiar.

Using nudges to move students past mental, emotional, and social blocks is an important tool in creating joyful experiences for students and setting them up for future successful educational opportunities.

Nudges Sorted by the Learning Triangle

The encouragement shown to President Obama by Buddy Guy, B.B. King, and Mick Jagger may not seem like advanced teaching pedagogy. Experienced teachers typically have an extensive repertoire of ways to encourage students past mental, emotional, and social blocks, whether or not they refer to them as nudges. When teaching and learning are going great, it can feel automatic to know what to say or do to move students forward in their learning.

However, when things are not going great, particularly when they are not going great to the extent that a teacher feels like quitting, thinking of and applying these nudges can be much more difficult. It can feel like an avalanche of bad class after bad class, creating a mountain of failure and tension that no amount of nudges can move.

Having a list of nudges that is frequently reflected upon and updated makes it easier to proactively and reactively respond to various teaching conditions and ensure student success. The following list of nudge ideas are sorted by the learning triangle so that teachers can determine which parts of the learning opportunity would have enough flexibility to be able to introduce a nudge when student effort, enthusiasm, or quality of work is waning. When a teacher notices students encountering mental, emotional, or social blocks, the teacher is ready with a mountain of nudges to keep the learning moving forward.

Engagement Nudges

Time. Carefully managing time can be effective in nudging students toward more engagement.

Limiting students' time on work can be helpful, particularly in creative work. Giving students a time limit changes the expectation from "this has to be a perfect, creative, incredible piece" to "show me the best you can do in two minutes and then there can be more opportunities to add to it later." In these instances, students may need to be told, "there is only 30 seconds left. No changing or adding to ideas now; you need to make what you have work." Paired with more open-ended work times, this nudges students to push past the emotional block of perfectionism to reach completed work that can flow through the design cycle of evaluation, re-design, and reiteration.

Elementary art teacher Jonathan Juravich (whom I introduced in the last chapter) often starts his art classes with a two-minute "quick draw challenge." In addition to "calming students' bodies" and getting their creative minds in gear, this activity is setting up an expectation that work in Jonathan's class does not have to be obsessed over to reach perfection. Ideas quickly put into action are celebrated. (One of Jonathan's quick draw ideas was "draw a vegetable with a mustache." Examples can be seen at www.adifferentedusite.com/timenudge.)

Nudging students to extend their time on a particular project can also be helpful. A timer could be used on a slide show to not allow the student to advance a particular slide for a given amount of time to give the student more thinking and reflecting time.

A timer in an open-ended exploration can be used to challenge students to move past superficial understandings. For example, if students are previewing a set of fiction books, a timer could be set before the students could sit down. After a superficial look, students might choose to stand up without further considering the books, but the standing nudge would probably cause many students to take a second look at the books while they were waiting to sit.

Performance. Cementing student work at a particular time and place elevates the effort and emphasis students put on the work. In performing arts classes, simply letting students know that this is "the performance" makes them approach the work more seriously, even if the only audience is the class. The aspect of performance can also be marked by recording students, even if the only audience will be the class watching themselves when the performance is over.

Note that "performance" is not limited to performing arts or live performances. Alison Nakasako, a French teacher at Bexley Middle School, had a "costume closet" made up of scrubs, a doctor coat, and even a wedding dress. Alison remarked that the costumes helped students "get into character" and "become someone else." The enduring nature of the activity caused many of her students remember those skits years later.

Lindsay Shankle and others in the language acquisition department at Bexley Middle and High Schools often utilize student "performances" to increase learning, engagement, and relationships. They often have students respond to prompts in the new language, recording their responses on the student video-sharing platform FlipGrid. Teachers can carefully listen to pronunciations to provide valuable feedback and all students have a chance to share things that are important to them with their teachers.

Novelty. An interesting, but unrelated concept can drive student engagement. This can be particularly effective in subject areas in which skill building requires a lot of repetition.

Nonon Mooney is a retired music teacher who spent most of her career teaching band, orchestra, and general music at Montrose Elementary. Beginning band and orchestra often require repetition to allow the teacher to make subtle adjustments to hand position, tone, etc. to establish a proper pedagogical foundation. Her novel approach to keeping engagement high was cow facts. Nonon recorded a series of novel, interesting facts about cows (i.e. "a cow has 32 teeth"). When she wanted to reward or encourage her students, she would announce, you have earned a cow fact and play the pre-recorded text from the cassette player set up in the front of the room.

When students needed an extra nudge, the cow facts were ready. Nothing in the learning triangle exists in a vacuum. This engagement strategy also created a class structure where students were able to connect with Nonon in a non-academic way. Soon her classroom was filled with cow items that students had brought into her, one of the prized gifts being a cow-themed chewing gum holder. As students saw their gifts displayed in the classroom, they were constantly reminded of the relationship that their teacher was interested in developing with them.

Competition. Competition can be an effective nudge to move students to a higher level of effort and intensity. Again, these nudges are designed to push students past blocks for learning opportunities they will enjoy. If students do not enjoy the activity to begin with, or only a select group of students enjoy it, introducing competition may have opposite of the desired effect. Likewise uneven competition, particularly when it becomes extremely difficult for one side to regain ground to win, can also become a nudge in the wrong direction. Conversely, when students enjoy the activity, even if they lose, there is still a positive feeling about the learning opportunity.

Competition can also be against oneself or against the past. A goal of "doing better than we did yesterday" is often enough of a nudge to increase effort and intensity.

For many years, my mom was a chaperone for a group of high schoolers at a weeklong summer camp. For several years, she was in charge of ten girls staying in a house with a single bathroom/shower. With a firm camp schedule that started early in the morning and ended late at night, time-efficient showers were important. To nudge the girls in that direction, my mom started the shower team. Each girl was tasked with taking a shower as fast as possible to get the teams overall time lower than the day before. What could have been a source of nagging, judgmental comparisons, and endless frustration became a fun game and lasting positive memory for the group. The girls even gave their shower team a name: the ducks.

Cooperation. Cooperation in the form of "group projects" tends to carry a negative connotation for many students. Yet there are many highly successful group projects occurring constantly at schools. They do not have the group projects label. They are called band, orchestra, choir, plays, musicals, the basketball team, the cheerleading squad, the debate team, etc. It would seem it is not the structure of a group project that makes it undesirable, but rather the content. When students enjoy doing something, they often enjoy doing it together.

If students do not find the task for the group project enjoyable to begin with, the cooperative aspect will probably not be an effective nudge. Often the group project becomes a game of academic chicken, with students judging who has the most to lose with a bad performance on the group task and then putting the bulk of the responsibility for the project on that person.

In contrast, in a joyful activity, the varying attention spans in a group offer an automatic catalyst for pushing through blocks. When one member's energy, focus, or creativity starts to drain, another member can continue to push through to the next stage of the work in which time the drained student is able to be refreshed and is able to stand in as other group members need refreshed.

Content Nudges

An obstacle to great teaching and learning is the student question "why do we have to learn/do this?" Content nudges are a way of framing the subject so that the answer to this question is more apparent to students all throughout the lesson.

Trans-disciplinary Projects. How do you get students to care about learning about Homer's *Odyssey*? In a unit originally assembled by Sara Hric and Rachel Braswel, New Albany High School teachers Jaqueline Loughry and Darryl Sycher utilized trans-disciplinary learning to show the book's timeless relevance. The course they were teaching, freshman humanities, already was a co-taught double-block integration of freshman language arts and freshman social studies. In the *Odyssey* unit, students also read excerpts from Jonathan Shay's *Odysseus in America: Combat Trauma and the Trials of Homecoming*. Shay's work displays the timeless nature of PTSD in soldiers by viewing Odysseus's reflections through the lens of post-traumatic stress disorder and comparing these reflections to the experiences of contemporary American soldiers.

This combination of studies allowed students to reimagine *The Odyssey* not as a perfunctory language arts requirement, but a reflection of timeless and current struggles, of which some students were personally familiar with. Analyzing Odysseus's actions now had clear relevance and function.

Issues and concepts are rarely as isolated in the real world as formal education tends to represent them. Trans-disciplinary learning represents issues and concepts more as they naturally occur and this often enables students to connect more deeply.

Purpose. "Because you are doing it for someone else." This is another way of answering, the "why do we have to learn/do this?" question. For Michael Vincent, a design teacher at Bexley Middle School, helping others is a requirement for design projects. Teachers across the district submit needs that they and their students have and he challenges his students to create designs and produce products for those students and teachers.

From a laptop holder to a movable multi-guitar stand to a tactile keyboard, students produce real-life products that make a difference to the people they are making them for. Knowing that their product would directly help someone else provided a powerful nudge for students to push past the minimal amounts of effort and time needed for a grade.

One student gave up extra "flex periods" for days to learn and apply the 3-D printing software needed to make her product. When the student realized that the 3-D printer would not be able to produce the size of product required, rather than giving up or stopping at a prototype, she continued to push forward, eventually coming up with the solution of printing several pieces that she then joined together.

When reflecting about the impact of these projects, Michael Vincent concluded, "The more students have time to engage with a stranger and discover that we have the power to improve someone else's life, the gifts back to the builder are incredibly gratifying."

Story. Any contemporary marketing professional will quickly let you know that "story" is the best way to communicate an idea. When a narrative is attached to an idea, it is easier for it to stick in listeners' minds. A wide variety of content can be set up as a narrative to humanize/personalize the material, clarify a timeline of events, and make concepts seem more applicable to real life.

The district that I am currently teaching in has deliberately looked for effective ways to teach students about racism. While the district has instituted a number of programs through the years, one of the most effective presentations occurred when Kim Rhodes (who was introduced in Chapter 2) shared her personal story of racism: growing up in a segregated city, having a bi-racial marriage, and navigating racism as a teacher of color in a predominantly white school district. When Kim gave the talk to the entire middle and high school student body, she had already established herself as a tough, but well-loved guest teacher that had had most, if not all, of the students in class. Suddenly issues of racism, redlining, and discrimination were not abstract, but personal, as seen in the experience of one of the students' beloved teachers. Story has an incredible impact. (For more on Kim's story and how she felt like quitting teaching during it, see Chapter 8.)

For young students, story can make directions easier to remember and more fun to follow. In the music classroom that I shared with Nonon Mooney (mentioned earlier in this chapter), we often had a set of thirty xylophones, glockenspiels, and metallophones set up in the back of the classroom. This made it easy to transition in and out of instrument playing. The "mallet pit" also was incredibly tempting for younger students to run and jump through during free movement activities. To avoid this, the area was filled with alligators that Nonon would call off when it was time to play the instruments. Even the youngest students recognized the fiction, but they loved trying to "spot" the vicious creatures among the instruments and they stayed out of that area when it was not time to play the instruments.

Social-Emotional Environment Nudges

Identity. Strongly associating with a particular identity can nudge students to raise their standards to that fit that identity. Uniforms and jerseys provide a powerful proof.

When I was in undergrad, I was a member of the Ohio State University Marching Band. Particularly in Ohio, the Ohio State University Marching Band has a strong reputation for excellence and precision. When I made the band, an athletic booster parent from my hometown told me that to him making the band was as good as making the university's Division 1 football team. When I walked across campus after football games, young children would routinely ask me to autograph their programs. This notoriety had nothing to do with my personal performance but was based on the tradition and identity associated with the band.

But it did affect the way I acted when I wore my band uniform. On several occasions, there was a band performance right after a scheduled class, so I wore my full uniform to class. At the end of one such class, a female co-ed noted, you look "cute" in your band uniform. With a suaveness that I rarely carried, I answered, "that's what I was going for." Whenever I walked across campus in my band uniform, I found myself standing taller, walking straighter, and carrying myself with an extra layer of poise and pride.

Clothing is a superficial marker of identity, but if even that makes a difference, how much more could teachers build students' identities with even stronger positive identity markers?

Flow/Schedule. Often without thinking about it, teachers are using a small nudge to get students to move into new learning opportunities. Just by keeping a schedule for the day, teachers are giving a nudge for students to move to the next activity rather than choose their own activity, which may or may not be conducive to further learning.

Purposeful transitions allow students to move easily into the next learning opportunity. Instead of "put your books away so we can get to this next activity," a teacher could say "when the video starts, as you are watching the video, put your books away and think about what character development is shown in this short clip, then be ready to tell me about it." When students don't know what will come next, they choose their own next activity. A simple nudge makes it clear where the class is heading and how the student can be part of that forward motion.

Nudges in the Wrong Direction

The nudges introduced so far have all been for the purpose of helping students to overcome mental, emotional, and social blocks. When teachers are not deliberate about designing content, engagement, and structure that reinforces student learning, it is easy for teachers to inadvertently give nudges in the wrong direction that create or enlarge mental, emotional, and social blocks.

Yes, And. In improvisation comedy, the scared maxim "yes, and…" is used to remind participants that allowing for possibility is what keeps the comedy going. Any negativity or questioning, while maybe garnering a quick laugh, will stifle the flow and not allow the actors to get to the bigger, more complex jokes that create longer scenes and captivated audiences. In the same way, any time a student shares a creative idea, you are given the opportunity to nudge them toward more engagement or less engagement. There are motivated, driven students that will continue to persevere despite nudges to disengage, but the students with the craziest ideas are often the ones that need the most constant positive nudges.

Fifth grade students were recently working in groups on a movement project in class. A student said, "I am planning to jump off the roof of the school and have my group members ready to catch me." Of course, this idea is not actionable. An option for me would be to tell him no, that doesn't work, think of something else. Or a more nuanced, yes, and approach might be:

> I like the excitement of jumping off the roof. We will need to limit the movement to the stage only. However, the video recording program we are using allows for backgrounds. Could you put together a background that makes it look like you are jumping off the roof?

I am thankful for the times that teachers utilized this "Yes, And" approach with me. I remember a particular incident when I was playing bongos on a roof in Spain. We were on a school-sponsored trip when I was in high school. Another student on the trip had purchased a set of Moroccan bongos and I was loving playing them. After 10–15 minutes of playing, the collection of chaperones and students also on the rooftop lounge area were not loving the bongo playing nearly as much as I was. Marilyn Shaw, a chaperone, who was also a veteran teacher at Wapakoneta City Schools, came over and gently asked me if I might try some softer sounds. As I began to play softer, she let me know how much she liked that playing style.

Marilyn's approach was effective. I moved to a much softer bongo playing style that was more agreeable with everyone on the roof. Since I was a junior in high school, I would like to think that I could have handled a much more direct approach.

Marilyn's "Yes, And..." approach was probably not only limited to rooftops in Spain; It certainly made an enormous difference in the daily interactions she had with her elementary students.

When a student asks, can I do x for this project? Or is y allowed? As much as possible, teachers should answer yes, and... to be able to further student creativity and engagement.

Delay and Lack of Follow-Up. When students are excited about receiving feedback or seeing a final product (edits for an essay, a specially formatted video, a matted piece of artwork, etc.), delay is a good way to extinguish the excitement and diminish enthusiasm for similar projects in the future. If the teacher needs to play a role in moving a project forward, be sure it is set up in a way that the teacher can communicate realistic time expectations to the students and follow through with them.

Complications. Online emergency teaching during the pandemic showed how easily students and especially parents can be nudged away from learning opportunities. When most of the United States was teaching online, social media platforms were full of memes describing the complicated list of instructions, passwords, and magical incantations parents and students felt they had to utilize to navigate the various platforms to view, complete, and turn in assignments. When students are in a space where teachers can give direct assistance, more complicated instructions can be endured more easily than online, but the lesson of simplicity learned from emergency pandemic teaching is a good one to hold on to.

Only the Beginning

This list is only the beginning of powerful, effective nudges that teachers use to further student learning. An expanded, live updating list of nudges, with examples and cited research, is available at adifferentedusite.com/nudges. The website allows teachers to dig into nudge ideas through search tools as well as submit their own examples.

How Do I Use This Tomorrow?

1. What instructional phrase(s) do you find yourself repeating over and over because students have trouble following it? How could you use a nudge for more efficiency (and less annoying of the teacher)?
2. Nudges can also work for teachers. What administrative type tasks are difficult for you to complete? What nudges could you use for yourself?
3. What other nudges do you use to move students past these social, emotional, and mental blocks? Share your ideas at adifferentedusite.com/nudges and see what other teachers are using as well.

How Do We Learn This Together?

#EduNudge. How have you used nudges in your classroom? The opposite of a nudge is a nag. Is there something that you have to keep reminding students about that you could replace with a nudge? Could you be brave enough to ask for help to come up with a nudge for this nag?

Nudges can have a powerful effect on student learning, becoming an important tool in maintaining great teaching and learning amid significant challenges. Not all nudges will always work for all students and teachers, so a careful reflection of what would work in your learning environment is vital. The availability of nudges that work for a teacher will be directly correlated to the strength of the learning structure that the teacher has established. Setting up and maintaining this successful learning structure is detailed next.

4

The Most Popular Classroom Management in the World

As shown in the learning triangle, when a teacher has great content, combined with effective engagement strategies, but the students are not learning, the structure of the learning environment needs to be examined.

In an ideal learning opportunity, the minimal levels of structure, combined with the objectives of the course are set up in a way to allow the maximum creative engagement from students.

This is seen in the popular classroom structure of a Massachusetts physical education teacher. His learning environment structure has been implemented and imitated all around the world with great success and acclaim.

One of his most famous lesson plans is a perfect example of matching engagement with content. He was working with strong young men so he wanted a game where the players could be very physical, but not aggressive. He wanted a game that involved a lot of players, but limited contact between players. He wanted to use a ball and goals, but to advantage skill over physicality, he set the goals high in the air with horizontal holes rather than vertical ones. This meant that more care would have to be taken in tossing the ball into the goals and the goals could not be easily blocked by an opponent. He wanted the game to be able to be played with minimal supervision, spreading beyond his class, so he kept the rules simple and straightforward. His lesson plans

DOI: 10.4324/9781003251330-5

met his content objectives and he carefully designed engagement to fit the students with which he was working.

But the lack of a structure conducive to learning in his classroom made his first trial of this lesson plan a complete disaster. By the end of the class a fight had erupted in the classroom; one student was unconscious, another student had a dislocated shoulder, and several other students had visible contusions.

He hesitated to try his lesson again but this PE teacher knew that he was on to something when his students begged him to bring back the game he had invented. He could see that his lesson would meet the desired objectives and that the students were motivated to establish a structure that would allow them to safely play the game.

He instituted more guidelines with clear, reasonable consequences if the expectations were not met. The second iteration of his game was a success. As his lesson plan went on to many more iterations with him and other instructors, the creativity of engagement within his original structure evolved and has continued to evolve for over 130 years. The PE teacher was James Naismith and the lesson plan was the game of basketball. Even though he probably felt like quitting with his very challenging group of original basketball students, he continued.

His school, Springfield College, has a stated objective of educating students in spirit, mind, and body for leadership in service to others. Millions of players, coaches, and parents all around the world can testify how the game of basketball has done exactly this.

James's basketball lesson provides a goal, hope, and vision for what great teaching and learning can be. James Naismith had set up an incredible learning opportunity with a classroom structure that not only kept students safe and engaged but provided the framework for students to develop the incredible degree of creative play that has come to define the game of basketball.

This is what an effective classroom structure is: a framework for student growth. As students grow in the objectives set forth in the lesson (whether academic, social, emotional), their growth is guided in a particular direction. The framework and structure are not the goal, but the means to the goal of the kind of Naismith-sized learning seen in the history of basketball. Students and teachers are working to establish the most open, creative, safe, welcoming, forgiving, interesting structure because this is what makes learning work.

Compliance, discipline, classroom management, and rules carry a negative connotation for some students and teachers. These learners have experiences in which compliance, discipline, and rules may have limited learning. Contrasted with the joy, wonder, and remarkable learning that come from classrooms in which students have a higher degree of freedom, it is tempting to decry any kind of rules and structure. But the structure and "classroom discipline" seen in the Naismith lesson were not an obstacle to great learning, they were the conduit of it.

In James's original lesson, perhaps some students enjoyed the free-for-all that ensued, but the joy was not universal. Just ask those students who got "punched in the clenches." With the minimum structure that James later established, all students were able to enjoy the lesson more equally. Creativity and innovation flourished by having a firm structure with which to grow in to and up through.

Structures in Growth and Gardening

This begins to look a lot like gardening. Recently, my mother purchased some large potted plants for my wife and I to put in our backyard. Sticking out of the two-foot pots were three-foot trellises. After a few months of growth, the flower plants began to grow up through the trellises.

The more you want something to grow in a certain direction, the more structure you need to supply to it. This does not hinder the growth. If done right, the structure encourages and maximizes the growth. Effective structures that teachers build in their classrooms provide guidance and space for growth while keeping everyone safe.

It can be easy to misjudge just what kind of "plants" we are growing as teachers. There have been times in my teaching career when I thought I was growing corn. With corn, you plant the seeds in the ground and the plant shoots straight up. When it's ready to be harvested, you can move very quickly through the field with a giant combine harvester without much concern of damaging the plants. If you really want to get higher yields, you can apply some fertilizer or pesticides, but the structure needed for a successful crop is minimal. Sometimes I had students that I thought would grow like corn. I expected them to grow in a specific direction with very little structure. I did not always give them the structure needed to grow in the ways that I wanted (and the curriculum demanded). They were frustrated and so was I.

As teachers, we are not growing corn. Mostly we are growing tomatoes. Tomatoes and corn are very different. Gardeners use trellises for tomatoes to keep them away from insects and provide more direct sunlight to all the plants. Then the tomatoes are carefully harvested by hand. The structure that a gardener provides to tomato plants increases their growth and sets it in a particular direction.

Structure and Safety

The structure for a classroom is defined by what is needed to keep students safe and lead them to grow in the direction defined by the curriculum. The ability to get to Naismith-sized learning is the criteria that classroom discipline decisions are made against. Is this a necessary structural element to be sure that students grow in the direction that the curriculum demands? If it is not necessary for their growth, it will probably just get in the way. Conversely, if students are not growing, is there some structure I am missing to guide their growth? It becomes very frustrating to students and teachers when the structure for the classroom is perceived as being too much or too little to engender learning.

Students want to be in a safe place and if the teacher is not providing a safe enough structure, the students will create that structure themselves, either by closing themselves off and shutting down or taking control of the classroom.

The fight that ensued during the first ever basketball game can be accurately seen as students seeking to take control of an unsafe classroom. Unfortunately, they took control in ways that were just as unsafe. Students need to know that the teacher can keep them safe physically or they will be ready to respond physically to threats.

Fortunately, most classrooms do not have a high degree of physical threats that need to be managed. However, *emotional injury and risk is a factor in all classrooms*. When a student is being emotionally harmed through a lesson, the injuries can be just as long-term as physical injuries, if not more so. It is very important that teachers are managing the level of emotional risk in the classroom, creating the emotional space that keeps students safe.

Just as physical space may be needed for students to stay safe, emotional space may be needed. In a creative writing class, students need to be able to share their work with the teacher to receive feedback and grow. There is a tremendous power in students getting this feedback from other students, but only if it can be done in a way that does not cause harm. If the feedback that students would give each other would cause harm, teachers need to re-evaluate the use of student-to-student feedback in the classroom. A teacher might need to suspend this kind of feedback to establish the minimum emotional space needed for student safety.

Minimum is a key concept here. Just as different levels of physical risk are acceptable in different settings and at different stages - consider high school football games vs. pre-school dance classes - different levels of emotional risk are acceptable as students become emotionally stronger. Often learning opportunities with a higher level of engagement involve more emotional risk, so there is a need to balance the risk and the rewards of these opportunities. It is important also to realize that age is not the same as maturity level and emotional strength can be very difficult to assess.

It is also important to remember that emotional strength can be affected by simple factors. When a student is well rested, with a full stomach, and appropriately hydrated, they are primed to be the strongest emotionally. When any of these are lacking, emotional risk is automatically higher.

Teachers can model emotional strength to students in powerful ways. While it is important that a teacher does not give the appearance of letting a student emotionally harm them, giving students space to freely express their frustrations without any risk of punishment from the teacher can be a valuable lesson and can disarm students who want to use put-downs and negative comments to the teacher as a way of manipulating the classroom environment. (Being strong enough emotionally that students can freely comment without bothering you demands emotional stability from other relationships, including teaching peers. More about this will be covered in Chapter 8.)

I was in a student–parent conference with a middle-school grade-level team. One of the special education teachers was addressing some of the behaviors that the student had been exhibiting. She turned to him and said, "okay, go ahead and call me whatever name you want. I promise, you won't get in trouble, no big deal." An enormous grin spread across the student's face.

"You're stupid," he said.

"Spell it and I'll be impressed," the intervention teacher immediately returned. The student had been effectively disarmed from trying to use his negative words to hurt the teachers or control the classroom.

Building Structure Through Embedded Expectations

One of the problems with James's initial approach to basketball is he had failed to ingrain the fundamental aspects of the school's expectations into the students. Knocking out students and "kicking and punching in the clenches" do not fit with "leadership in service to others."

However, as James found out, class expectations don't need to be treated as a separate curriculum, but rather can be embedded into the content that the students are ready to engage with. To teach cooperation, James didn't give a lecture on cooperation with a follow-up worksheet; rather, he changed the rules (prohibiting moving with the ball) to require more cooperation. To set up the expectation of non-violence, he didn't require them to complete online modules about non-violence, he put in a consequence of the other team earning points if a team became violent. He taught non-retaliation by awarding a team a point if they were fouled three times in a row by the opposite team. If teams immediately retaliated after a foul, no points were awarded.

A game setting clearly lends itself to embedded expectations, but expectations can be embedded into any content.

Kim Rhodes' "word of the day" mentioned in Chapter 3 could be adapted to become an embedded class expectations lesson in a language arts class by having students define words like "synergy," "reciprocity," and "altruism." As students worked together and a master teacher guided their work, they would be demonstrating these very concepts. Antonyms like "dissidence," "caustic," "egocentric" and some play acting could also be used to come up with counter examples.

An embedded expectation in a math class might involve students given statistics on cooperative learning, positive feedback, or other classroom expectations and the students could work in groups to convert them to ratios and fractions to represent them in different ways. They would be learning about cooperation and doing it at the same time.

Starting a course with an embedded expectations lesson shows that the expectations for the class are not an abstract concept that is considered when something goes awry, but a necessary structure for making the class work. And by introducing the expectations right away, you can hopefully avoid most of the "punching in the clenches." (For additional examples of embedded expectations, see adifferentedusite.com/blog.)

Building Structure Through Earning

Establishing a structure conducive to Naismith-sized learning is a process. Students have to be strong enough mentally, socially, and emotionally to grow through these structures. It is often difficult to tell how strong students are in these areas. Student levels of strength can be determined by testing and earning.

In one of my first days of student teaching, I was very excited to re-create a lesson that I had seen in my general music methods class. We were going to be playing and improvising with the minor blues scale on the classroom xylophones. In the methods class full of musicians with decades of experience, we were grooving and jamming with very little instruction given.

In the fifth-grade class I taught, the room soon fell to chaos as I sent them to get instruments and start playing. The lesson plan was full of great content and very engaging, but, like James, I had failed to structure the classroom in a way that made learning work.

Nonon Mooney, whom I had mentioned earlier with her novelty and story nudges, was at this point my cooperating teacher. She told me to make the students "earn" playing the xylophones. Before having students move to an instrument that they can use in a very loud and distracting manner, each student had to demonstrate to me they could "air-play" the pattern we would be doing on the xylophones. Once I saw a student correctly air-playing the part, they were dismissed to the instruments. Having the students "earn" the opportunity to play by air-playing the pattern cleared up most of the chaos and we were replicating the success of the college methods class quickly.

Any preferred component of a learning experience can be used as an opportunity to have students practice and demonstrate the needed structure of the class. If students are going to use laptops to write the first drafts of their essays, perhaps they need to leave encouraging post-its about other students' work before they can open their laptops. Before going outside to work on math problems on a sunny day, perhaps students need to complete the first five problems and check them with a neighbor.

Like James, Nonon knew that if students preferred an activity, they would be very willing to meet simple, clear class expectations to be able to participate in the activity. This will allow all students to cooperatively engage in joyful learning.

Building Structure Through Relationships

Structure is a combination of the physical and emotional aspects of the classroom that create an environment where students feel safe and confident to take risks and move forward in their learning. As seen in the Jonathan Juravich example from Chapter 2, relationships are a huge part of this.

Once a teacher has established a warm relationship with students, it is easier for them to feel comfortable and take on risks in their learning. It is difficult to understate the significance of the relationship between the teacher and the students on the learning environment.

At the very beginning of a course/year, this relationship may not be that warm or established. It is also possible that things may happen during the year that cause the relationship levels to rise and fall (more about this in Chapter 7). In those cases, teachers can also utilize the relationships students have or can form with each other.

Putting students into pre-defined small groups at the very beginning of a course can be a great way to utilize these peer relationships. There is an identity formed in the group that helps pull along students that may not have originally connected with the teacher. There may also be students that already have positive relationships with each other that can be built upon.

Although I think I am a very connectable person, if I also give students the opportunity to connect with three other students in the room, the chances of the connection happening and happening quickly are essentially tripled. As noted in the previous chapter, group work does not work well for non-preferred activities, but students sharing activities that they enjoy is the very definition of bonding. This sets up the class not only for that particular learning opportunity, but students now have positive relationships with other students in the class as well as the teacher.

Building Structure Over Time

This classroom structure is not a destination that the class arrives at. Classroom management is not even the journey, but rather the first step on a journey of classroom cultivation leading to the Naismith-sized learning we all dream of.

This long-term view also allows teachers flexibility and patience in responding to student actions. If there is not an immediate safety threat (physical or emotional), the consequences of a student's actions do not have to be immediate. This needs to be reiterated. A teacher does not need to respond immediately to all off-task behaviors. There are many times when a teacher's immediate response to behaviors should only be safety-related. If there is a large emotional component to the behavior and the confrontation, the student will probably not be able to experience any learning until they have calmed down.

A teacher may find that a class's response to a learning opportunity simply means that they do not have a classroom structure strong enough to be able to sustain that task. Punishment is rarely needed or effective, but simply the consequence is that additional structure needs to be in place before that learning opportunity can be given again. Given that students are physically and emotionally safe, a short-term victory in compliance is not a victory at all if it does not continue to build a warm, inclusive classroom environment.

A teacher may also find that the class's behavior may be communicating their preferred learning style for the day. At times I have been frustrated by a class in which I am constantly telling them to stop talking. On my best days, rather than continuing to frustrate myself and my students pushing for their silent compliance, I make my explanations as fast and simple as possible and move them into activities where they can talk to each other. This often means that some students will be confused about the activity. Since they are in a mood to talk, often other students are ready to sit alongside them and figure it out together. My lesson objective is never to have students listen to me. If students are in a mood to talk to each other, they may be ready to experience much deeper learning than would happen if they were just listening to me.

If James Naismith had tightened the regulations for the basketball game to the point that there was no chance of any physical contact and injury, he would have gotten through another class, but the game would not have come to be defined by the open-ended creativity that it has today.

Defining Long-Term Success: An Unusual Dessert Song

For an entire year, I had a student that I failed at engaging in music class. For the purpose of this story, I will refer to him as Jamie. Jamie sat at the back of the room every class, often with his head down, sometimes moaning and crying in general frustration. At times it was disruptive to the rest of the class and all the time it was difficult for me to continue with anything when I knew I had a student in distress. Yet, despite what I tried, the environment never progressed to a point where he felt like engaging.

I had the student again the next year. For reasons mostly unrelated to that particular student, I made some massive structural changes to my class. I had gotten a grant for a classroom set of computers that students could utilize for more independent, self-paced work. In Jamie's class, I also had a co-teacher, Jason Hogue, who was a professional guitarist and bassist.

The class started out the same as the year before. Jamie was often upset and not engaged with the content. However, at times when students were working more independently with the devices, I could work one on one with Jamie without neglecting the other students. Because the other students were doing music tasks on the laptops with headphones, if Jamie was upset, he would not distract from their work. Jason, my co-teacher, also began to work one on one with Jamie. Jason found that Jamie was full of creative ideas and the two of them made a dynamic songwriting team.

Slowly, an emotional structure began to form that we could build some learning on to. Jamie was starting to get excited about bringing his ideas for songs and music into reality. This actually increased the frustration and what might be perceived as "negative behaviors." As Jamie began to take more risks and the rewards became palpable, not getting to the rewards became even more frustrating to him. Sometimes there were really large outbursts. Jamie would be screaming at top volume with tears coming down his cheeks. What is more preferable - a student yelling with tears streaming down his cheeks because he can't remember how to use the recording software to record his song or a quiet student in the back that never raises his head?

I am not claiming that this had to be a binary choice. I would like to think that with more skills, creativity, and experience we could have gotten to deep learning without these emotional outbursts, but these outbursts were much easier to handle knowing that we all were making progress and the frustration reflected the learning that was happening for Jamie. It is also significant to note that while most students found the songwriting in my class very engaging, only a few were achieving Jamie's level of creativity, iteration, and polish.

The level of emotional safety that Jamie had reached by the end of the course was evident when Jason accompanied Jamie singing his original song in front of the class. Added to that, I was later doing a workshop at the local library, bringing in a variety of student and professional musicians to demonstrate improvisation and creative music making. I asked Jamie to sing. The student that would not lift his head in music class was now sharing his unique song about insect-based desserts with total strangers.

I wish that I would have had the creativity and resources to create a structure that worked for Jamie the first year I had him in class. But I am also thankful that rather than settling and demanding some sort of perfunctory compliance, Jason and I were able to reach a little bit of the Naismith-sized learning we are all looking for.

How Do I Use This Tomorrow?

1. Are there any aspects of your classroom structure that are unnecessary for student learning? If you can't think of any, ask your students. You don't have to agree with them, but they might have some aspects worth considering revising.

2. Are there any places where your students need more support to grow in the direction the curriculum requires? These could be academic, social, or emotional standards.

3. Do you have any lesson ideas that you were really excited about but did not seem to work? Perhaps it is worth re-examining these ideas and seeing if adding more structure (like James Naismith did) might be the answer. Think about the specific point in the lesson when things went awry. Could you add structure there that would reinforce the expectations of the learning space needed for learning?

How Do We Learn This Together?

#NaismithSizedLearning. How has focusing on student learning rather than student compliance creating Naismith-sized learning in your classroom? What classroom management/rule compliance issues might you try to get rid of to make more room for independent learning?

The time and creativity it takes for teachers to build these effective structures on top of creating effective content and engagement are significant. Even when things are going well, managing time becomes another reason that teachers feel like quitting. In the next chapter we'll look at approaches to managing this prep and planning time effectively.

5

You Don't Have to Spend Your Weekend Planning (But You Can)

Often when teachers begin to teach, the passion and drive for great teaching and learning can become consuming. Whether it is getting carried away in the process or a deep commitment to the students, many teachers plan, prepare, and respond to lessons for as long as necessary to get the desired learning outcomes. Many teachers routinely work outside the bounds of the teaching contract. These efforts are regularly applauded and celebrated.

I never had a student teaching supervisor or administrator suggest to me that I consider the balance between my preparation time and the student activity time as a primary consideration for materials until many years into my teaching. Dr. Fred Hammond of Ashland University had been brought in as a professional development speaker at Bexley City Schools to teach about visual thinking routines. In the middle of his presentation, he offhandedly mentioned that he had to keep reminding student teachers he was working with that they needed to make sure they were spending far less time preparing for the learning opportunities than the students were spending participating in the learning opportunities. Evaluating a learning opportunity based on the ratio of time it takes to assemble (and respond to) over the time students participate in the activity never dawned on me. This assembly to activity ratio has since become an important part of my planning and time management strategy.

DOI: 10.4324/9781003251330-6

Even if teachers can manage a more time-consuming approach for a while, it is likely that at some point in a 30+ year career the teacher will have additional priorities in their life competing with the massive amounts of time they are spending prepping, preparing, and responding to students. When teaching is very time consuming and there are other life priorities not being fulfilled, teachers feel like quitting.

Finding the time to be able to sustainably manage all of the demands of teaching is not always a problem that can be solved exclusively by the teacher. Moreover, regardless of whether a teacher feels like quitting, most teachers would be able to positively affect students learning with more open and flexible time. To every extent that is possible, teachers should be advocating for more open, flexible time, then using the time to creatively meet student needs and advance student learning, showing administrators and stakeholders the possibilities and positive effects of such approaches.

This kind of advocacy often does not produce quick or dramatic schedule changes. If teachers are given a little more open, flexible time and show results in student learning, more small, incremental changes may occur. While schedule changes resulting in more open, flexible time are slow, teachers that do not communicate how they are taking advantage of open and flexible time quickly lose it.

Regardless of the amount of time and flexibility a teacher is given, using the time efficiently by being aware of the assembly to activity ratio can lead teachers to a more manageable and sustainable teaching practice.

To decrease the assembly to activity ratio, a teacher can either decrease the top number (the amount of time spent preparing a learning opportunity) and/or increase the bottom number (the amount of time students constructively spend on an activity). To examine what this would look like, here is the tale of two teachers on a day in which they were both achieving a small ratio of assembly to activity. Mr. Brown is a third-grade teacher and Ms. Smith is a high school math teacher. While these accounts are fictional, they are based on an aggregate of experiences from colleagues and my own teaching.

Template Activities, Student Independence, Student-Created Work

Mr. Brown begins his third-grade class with a lyric dictation from one of their favorite songs. Today the class is listening to "Roar" by Katie Perry, chosen by Deanna. Yesterday while the class was completing this same activity with a different song, Mr. Brown sat down with Deanna and helped her choose a song, copy the lyrics to a doc, create blanks for students to listen for, and create a few comprehension questions about the song. While the students are listening multiple times to the song to fill in the missing words and answer the comprehension questions Deanna wrote, Mr. Brown is preparing the next day's song with Mateo.

Mr. Brown is using *template activities*, doing the same kind of learning opportunity with different material. Because the students know what to expect, after a few rounds, the students can work very independently. Mr. Brown is also utilizing *student-created work*. Rather than picking a song himself and creating comprehension questions, Mr. Brown is having the students create the lyric sheet, including printing copies for the class on the classroom printer. This activity provides students with reading practice in several areas - fluency (repeated readings at a set pace), comprehension, and vocabulary. Because this is a preferred activity for students, they are very engaged and work hard to make sure the activity can continue so everyone in the class will be able to take a turn leading the activity. This activity takes virtually no additional planning time because Mr. Brown is able to utilize the time freed up by the independent work his students are doing.

Ms. Smith begins her morning Algebra class having them log in to the class's website and checking out the story problems created by the afternoon Algebra class the day before. The classes take turns posting problems on a discussion board and then checking each other's answers at the beginning of class. While this approach took some preparation at the beginning of the year, students now enjoy trying to stump the other class with tricky questions and leaving inside jokes within the story problems.

Ms. Smith is also utilizing *template activities and student-created work*. Ms. Smith uses the time the students are working independently to check out the report from the self-grading homework from the night before. Based on the student responses, she either works individually with students or creates a mini lesson if several students are missing the same concept.

Collaboration

Mr. Brown continues his language arts block with a phonics activity that another third-grade teacher in his building developed. Mr. Brown is using this activity from his colleague and his colleague will be using one of Mr. Brown's math activities later in the day. When Mr. Brown and his colleagues share lesson plans, they prepare everything for each other - making copies and collecting supplies for both classes at once to maximize the efficiency of their prep time.

For second period, Ms. Smith is able to collaborate with the other geometry teacher in the district. Ms. Smith loves to make silly videos of her and her cat explaining math concepts. Her colleague, Mr. Lopez, who took a course last spring on using adaptive quizzing software, creates online quizzes with question banks and adaptive links to the videos that Ms. Smith made. Mr. Lopez's and Ms. Smith's class both benefit from both teachers' expertise and collaboration. It also means more materials produced in less time for both classes.

Reusing Student Work

When Mr. Brown's students return from morning recess, they tour the hallway which is lined with some animal infographics that third graders made last year. Students spend ten minutes looking at the infographics and leaving sticky notes about what they liked about the infographics and what features of the infographics made the information easier to learn. Once again, Mr. Brown teamed up with his third-grade teaching colleague. She selected several great projects from last year and printed them, then Mr. Brown put them up in the hallway. When Mr. Brown's class is done doing the "gallery walk," the other third-grade class will complete the same activity.

With very little time put in on the teachers' end, the students are provided with lots of examples of what they will want to include in the infographics they are making. This pre-planning reflection time makes a big difference in the quality of work the students produce. By using authentic exemplars instead of teacher-created examples, the students have a clear idea of what is feasible and expected for their work.

My high school Spanish teacher at Waynesfield-Goshen High School, Marcia Pepple, had yearly end of course projects we would complete to demonstrate our Spanish language skills and understanding of Spanish and Latin American cultures. Before and/or during the project she would show us examples from previous years of great work that former students had completed. The time we spent looking at the exemplars was not only teaching us how to do the project, but also teaching about the cultural topics the projects were covering.

Ms. Smith's fourth period Statistics class is beginning a several-weeks-long project in which the students will produce videos utilizing statistics to communicate a social concern. The project involves green screens, advanced video-editing software, and spreadsheet/data analysis software. Ms. Smith knew her students would be very excited about a practical application of their learning, but the project also required skills in which Ms. Smith was not very strong. To prepare, Ms. Smith taught a summer course in which students at a nearby community college completed a similar, but less involved project. Not only does Ms. Smith already have exemplars from her summer course to show to the class, she got paid to plan, prepare, and troubleshoot for the project she is now doing with her students.

National and Worldwide Collaboration

After lunch recess, Mr. Brown continues the read aloud *Front Desk*. Students are not only actively listening to the story, but also thinking about what questions they might ask their twitter pen pals. When Mr. Brown started reading the book, he noticed that a teacher at an American school in Singapore posted that his class was reading the same book. Mr. Brown and the Singapore teacher began a video pen pal collaboration. After each chapter, each class thought of questions to ask each other about the book. The students send videos back and forth, both individually and as a class.

Aubrey Smalls is a celebrated music teacher in Chesterfield County Public Schools in Virginia. When I saw a video he had posted on Twitter with him playing "Jingle Bells" on the tenor saxophone with his music students, I knew my students would also enjoy the video. I shared it with my students. My students and I then added a class percussion and drum set part and sent it back to Aubrey and his class. Aubrey responded that his students enjoyed our response. All students enjoyed realizing they were jamming with a class halfway across the country. This led to a second collaboration on "Dreidel, Dreidel," complete with xylophones, a jumping prep exercise, and more tenor saxophone and drum set.

Twitter, Facebook, Instagram, and other social media platforms are great sources for finding exemplars and connecting with other teachers and students. Collaboration can come from down the hall and across the world.

Doing Only What Only You Can Do

To be able to maximize independent student work time, Mr. Brown has his students using many computer applications that they are first experiencing in his class. In third grade, there is a wide range of computer experience to begin with and the use of all these programs can get intense for his students. To not be overwhelmed by the student frustrations, and to teach students about patience, focus, and determination, Mr. Brown often has a five-minute interval after giving instructions during which he does not answer any student questions. While at first students were frustrated at not finding immediate answers, they now notice that they can work together and figure out almost all the technical issues by asking each other and not waiting for Mr. Brown.

This allows Mr. Brown to only deal with advanced technical issues that need administrative support or focus exclusively on academic support rather than technical computing support.

Ms. Miller applies the same approach to math instruction support. The last ten minutes of class are set aside for students to begin their homework and Ms. Miller to provide individualized instruction. To incentivize students helping each other, students get double credit if they help another student and document their diagnosis of the misconception. That means if a student helps other students, they only might have to do half the number of problems. Even if students try to game the system by faking mistakes to each other, Ms. Miller counts it as a win that students are demonstrating a deep understanding by pointing out common misconceptions. With most students getting help from each other, Ms. Miller can be very strategic about which students she helps. Also a win: the more students that take advantage of this setup, the less grading Ms. Miller has to do.

After-School Differentiation

It's 4:30 on Friday night of the fourth week of school. Ms. Miller has rushed home to change into her school-color coordinated spirit wear and head to the home football game. She is not a coach of any kind, or on the band staff, or involved in any official compacity, but she just enjoys watching the football games, talking to students, parents, and other teachers while cheering on the team, band, and cheerleaders.

Mr. Brown is still in the hallway outside of his room, carefully constructing a display of the animal infographics that his third-grade class put together over the past week. In addition to matting each of the students' infographics, he has designed and printed individual labels for the students work. The labels include the student's name and the encouraging message "this infographic expertly designed by the young zoologist _____." The display is striking and will certainly draw parents, teachers, and other students to examine and interact with the work his students have created.

Each of these teachers is putting time and energy outside of the school day into activities that will certainly increase student engagement and achievement. In the middle of math class on Monday when one of her students seems overwhelmed because the concepts seem too complicated, Ms. Miller turns to the student and says "hey, great run in the fourth quarter for that touchdown. If you can block defenders and run for a forty-yard touchdown, I know you got this."

As Mr. Brown's students file in they will be scanning the hall to find their work and take an extra second to look back at Mr. Brown as they find their infographic and see the encouraging message he has printed on each matted project. Ms. Miller and Mr. Brown's principals should make it a point to acknowledge the time and effort each one them spent pouring into their students outside of the school day.

In both instances, however, it is important that Ms. Miller and Mr. Brown differentiate their prep time with their volunteer time. Both Ms. Miller and Mr. Brown enjoy spending time on these activities outside of the school day. It is interesting to them and when Ms. Miller and Mr. Brown walk into the building on Monday, they are excited to see the students because of the extra time they have put in outside of the school day.

But because these are volunteer hours, the next weekend, Ms. Miller finds that Friday night is going to be the only time that she will be able to spend with her sister before her sister moves to a new city so Ms. Miller skips the football game. Mr. Brown's car started making weird noises and Friday after school was the soonest he could get an appointment. So for the next week's display, Mr. Brown will simply staple up work the students did, spending five minutes at the end of his planning block instead of staying for an hour after school.

Proactively identifying what is required and volunteered allows a teacher to change course and adjust if they are feeling overwhelmed and other priorities are limiting the time a teacher can spend. There are all sorts of volunteer activities - hobbies, interests, passions - that teachers have that can transfer to increased student learning. There is no need for teachers to stop doing these things just because they are not paid for it, but teachers need to be able to re-focus and minimize volunteer activities when these activities get in the way of other priorities.

It is also important to be relentless about determining what volunteer activities actually increase student learning. When a teacher is volunteering their time, the effect on student learning can be secondary to the interest level and joy the teacher finds in the activity. This means that one teacher might want to spend a lot of time doing something that another teacher never does. And because we acknowledge the inherent differences between people, there is no guilt or shame for the teacher that volunteers in one way that another teacher does not.

There is a series of videos online by an elementary teacher named Mr. DeMaio. He and some of his friends create multiplication fact parodies of popular songs. I know that for students in my classes his videos have increased student learning. It also looks like the videos were a lot of fun to produce. If Mr. DeMaio and his friends enjoy making videos, why shouldn't they put this interest and joy toward something that also benefits students? At the same time, there might be a teacher down the hall from Mr. DeMaio that never creates videos. He might find that he actually sees a similar increase in student learning because he loves to watch professional basketball and he finds out that many of the students in his class do too. The ratio of student achievement raised in relation to the time and energy put in might be similar for both teachers. And because both activities are volunteer, the teachers need to feel the freedom to start and stop whenever other priorities take precedence.

Decrease Volunteer Grading

Even grading can become a "volunteer activity." Most, if not all, schools require teachers to evaluate students and report grades, but most schools do not have a specific amount of grading that needs to be done, specifically in the early practice/development stages of a unit. It is worth asking how detailed grading really needs to be.

Ms. Miller never grades all the math problems she assigns. A quick check shows if students have done the work and then

Ms. Miller randomly picks to grade the even or odd problems. If she notices a student is not understanding a concept, she doesn't bother grading more than 2–3 problems; rather, she spends the time thinking about what intervention to utilize with the student. Ms. Miller's homework scores are only used for planning purposes. She has unit tests and projects that determine a students' letter grade for the class.

Mr. Brown utilizes the 1:1 computers in his room as much as possible to be efficient in grading. Spelling tests, multiple choice tests, and even first drafts are all "graded" by the computer. Utilizing random question banks, students can re-take these assessments on their own when they feel ready. Mr. Brown has also most of his work set up in modules so there are specific assessments students must complete at a certain level before moving on to preferred digital activities. This means that most of the time students are coming to him to complete their missing work; he does not have to keep track of them.

Student Ownership of Learning

One of the key aspects of many of the components of Ms. Miller's and Mr. Brown's Day is students taking ownership of their learning. When students want to learn and are given the freedom to direct the learning, often guided with a nudge, the teacher has far less work to do and the students are probably going to do better also.

When I was eight years old, my grandparents sold their house to tour the country in a motor home. This also involved a large auction of many items that my grandparents could not take in the RV and did not want to put in storage. I attended the auction and managed to score an incredible buy: a full set of *Encyclopedia Britannica* from the 1960s. While my parents were probably not excited about finding a home for the 30+ volume set, I was ecstatic.

One of the auxiliary volumes to the encyclopedia was a translation dictionary. Thousands of words were translated into half a dozen different languages. This was a tremendous source of learning for me. I started out just looking up words for fun, comparing different languages. At one point, I put together a secret command list for my imaginary special ops team. Each command came from different languages I had never heard of to confuse any non-team members that might be infiltrating the communications.

Once I had a great resource in my hands, I did not require any supervision for creative learning to occur. I believe this is a universal quality of learning. As we make teaching students to be independent, creative learners a primary goal, the closer students get to that goal, the less we need to prepare and plan. And most of the time, the more students will get out of the learning opportunities.

How Do I Use This Tomorrow?

1. What specific tasks take up outside of contract time for you? Are these required tasks or volunteer? If there is any question, arrange a time to talk to your principal/supervisor to determine what is required versus suggested or appreciated. What plans can you make to limit out of contract time for volunteer activities, even when you enjoy them?

2. How can you shift your grading from a focus on quantity to quality? What specific assignments benefit from in-depth assessment and analysis with the student and which assignments can get automatic feedback or assessment from other students?

3. In what ways can you collaborate with colleagues in your building and district? Are there ways you could start a collaboration without their permission (online recordings, concerts, resources, etc.)?

4. What student-created work could you utilize in class? Could your students create their own Kahoot games? Review questions? Quizlets?

How Do We Learn This Together?

#AssemblyActivityRatio. What strategies do you use to lower the assembly to activity ratio? What tasks are taking up lots of time that you would like to lower the ratio for?

Most of the other aspects of achieving a small assembly to activity ratio are based on having positive and collegial relationships with other teachers and the principal/administrative teams. This is not always easy and will be covered in the next chapter.

6

How and Why to Ignore Standardized Testing

For many teachers, standardized testing is a reason they feel like quitting teaching.

A fifth-grade teacher was explaining to me why one of her students was having trouble participating in music class. We happened to be doing a lot of clapping that day and I had failed to notice that this student's hands were red and sore from chemotherapy treatments. I felt terrible. With tears in her eyes, the teacher concurred, telling me about the difficulties of the hours-long paper and pencil standardized test for the student that she had to administer.

This is why teachers feel like quitting because of standardized testing. Many times, the balance between the importance placed on standardized testing and the reality of the organic, multi-faceted nature of children is very off.

In this instance above, I am not sure about all of the factors in play. I am not sure where the directive for the testing was coming from. I do know that the testing had already been delayed several times. I do know that even if an administrator had exempted her from the test or she had chosen to opt out, this might also have created problems as these tests are used to determine placement in advanced courses. This student might not have been able to continue with the accelerated coursework she had been taking. Or it might have been that the student wanted to just "be normal" and take the test, even though it was painful. It seems

DOI: 10.4324/9781003251330-7

like everyone was stuck in a less than ideal, frustrating situation with no good alternatives.

When things like this happen over and over again, with little or no empathy from administrators, parents, legislators, or other stakeholders, teachers feel like quitting. It can feel like the day-to-day experiences and observations that teachers have about student growth are eclipsed by sets of arbitrary numbers. Being around students for hours each day, teachers are very aware of the unpredictable, organic, non-linear nature of student growth that does not always get reflected on a standardized test. When the process and results of tests are organized, processed, interpreted, and acted on with little or no acknowledgement of this nature, students are affected. While there is a strength and power in standardized data, there are also ways that standardized data erases context and misses important information.

Putting Data in the Right Context

When I was in first grade, my teacher had a homework assignment where we would be given a small piece of paper with six random words on it. We were to practice reading the words at home, then come back the next day and read them back to her. Every afternoon she would sit at the iconic kidney-shaped reading table and call us up to recite our homework words. If we didn't practice the night before or we just didn't want to do it, we could choose to skip our turn that day. Due to a combination of my poor reading skills and my preference for spending my class time drawing planes and ships, I almost always skipped my turn.

Somewhere around the middle of the year, I looked at my classmate's homework paper. I had no idea what the words on his paper said. The number on his paper was #117 and mine was #7. This data looked very simple. My 7 was on one end of the number line and Matt's 117 was on the other. Without context it would have been easy to apply labels to each end; Matt is smart and I am stupid. (Figure 6.1)

I'm not sure what all kinds of data the school was assembling, but by the middle of my second grade year, any additional data gathered were telling the same story. I was not reading at

FIGURE 6.1 Linear Comparison of Reading Scores.

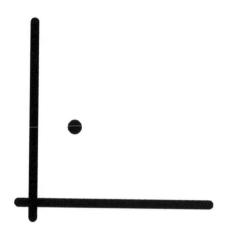

FIGURE 6.2 Teeth Development and Reading Scores.

the level that many of my peers were and I was not reading at the level I was expected to be reading at. The school let my parents know. My mother, who was also a teacher, worked with me at home, utilizing a progressive reading curriculum.

This is where context started to matter. As my mom worked with me, I overheard her say something, maybe to me or just loud enough that I could hear it. She commented that she had heard of reading being related to teeth development. She said, once your adult teeth come in, this will probably all clear up. This was important because it took the data from a one-dimensional line graph to a two-dimensional coordinate plane. There was another variable here. It no longer was as simple as Matt is smart and I am stupid (Figure 6.2). An even more accurate model would be a 3-D rendering with an additional axis of motivation/ engagement. (Figure 6.3). If the math existed, a myriad of factors would be mapped together, creating a full picture of who I was as a student and how that was intersecting with the specific scores I was getting on the assessments. This multi-dimensional landscape would reveal how my growth in other areas – motivation, focus, perhaps even dental development, would affect my reading.

My mom's approach made it appropriately difficult for me and others involved to apply the one-dimensional labels of smart and stupid to my learning. My mom did not approach only my first-grade reading challenge this way. This reflected the attitude she had always shown me and all her students. Her putting the data in a broader context meant that neither I nor her intervention students had an easy time putting ourselves on that line graph and thinking we were stupid.

All of our students are multi-dimensional learners because they are human beings, not test-taking machines. The scores that they receive in a particular moment are a beautiful mash-up of their achievement, experiences, feelings, mood, motivation, and inspiration at that particular time. This raw information is important, but not complete.

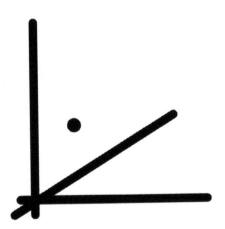

FIGURE 6.3 Teeth Development, Reading Score, and Engagement/Motivation.

The Myth of Linear Progress

For most teachers and students, data collection and analysis have progressed beyond a one-dimensional number line. This gives more accurate and useful information, but also produces different types of misconceptions about student learning.

Linear progress is a way of describing the expectation that growth will steadily continue. Mathematically, linear expressions are defined by the form $y = mx + b$. This means that at the starting place, b, the value (y) will rise at a constant rate of m. In non-mathematical terms, imagine riding a bike straight up a ramp at a constant speed, each second taking you a little bit higher. To illustrate the limits of linear progress, consider how specific this description had to be. Climbing a ladder has vertical progress, but it is not steady as weight is shifted from foot to foot and hand grasps are adjusted and re-adjusted. Climbing rocks has vertical progress, but often a horizontal move is needed for a better footing, making the vertical progress uneven.

These details in distinctions might seem unimportant when talking about going up a ladder or climbing rocks, but in learning it is important that students and teachers know what to expect in the learning process. If students, parents, and teachers expect to continue to keep getting better and better and smarter and smarter, times of less growth may greatly alarm them. If the expectation is for growth to be steady and constant, bad days can seem fatal and low test scores carry catastrophic and outsized meanings.

Imagine climbing up a mountain. If two people are climbing two different mountains and the only way you have to assess their progress is their altitude, it would be hard for there to be any meaningful comparisons. One mountain might have treacherous terrain at the bottom – thick brush that is time consuming to beat through. The other mountain might have a manicured path leading far up it, making the progress quick and effortless. Thinking about climbing a mountain, not only does a linear evaluation of altitude not show where the climbers really are, it gives misleading information on the relative progress of each climber. Even further, it may distort the climbing potential of each climber. The best we can do is try and understand the particular mountain that a student might be climbing and the obstacles they might be facing, then apply interventions to overcome those obstacles.

There are few, if any, things in life in which linear progress is expected. Sprinting can be measured very linearly, yet elite runners do not and are not expected to run a faster race every single time they run. These are adults spending all of their time and basing their livelihood on running as fast as they can. And still sometimes they don't improve. If a mature Olympic-level athlete with a singular focus on results cannot achieve this constant linear progress, we cannot expect a second grader concurrently developing academically, socially, and physically to be able to achieve this either.

The Trends That Trend Lines Represent

Trend lines are an important facet of the linear progress myth. For a number of standardized tests, after students take the assessment, a constant linear trend line is drawn of their expected progress through the year. I remember my daughter taking reading assessments in elementary. Her scores were steadily rising, following and even exceeding the trend line, when suddenly, the scores fell. The raw data indicated a need for drastic interventions. However, when my wife and I looked at the data, we realized that the night before that last assessment, we had had a family emergency. My daughter had been quickly shuttled to our friends' apartment while we spent most of the night at the hospital. It is not surprising that in the emotional turmoil following that night, my daughter's reading score fell. She is not a one-dimensional test taking machine. She is a human being.

It bears shouting over and over again – these trend lines are only useful in showing long-term growth with a multitude of data points. When a straight trend line is drawn, it means that the chart could look like Figures 6.4–6.6, or something else entirely. All of these data points create the same trend lines. These are all normal for learning because children are not one-dimensional test taking machines. They are human beings that are affected

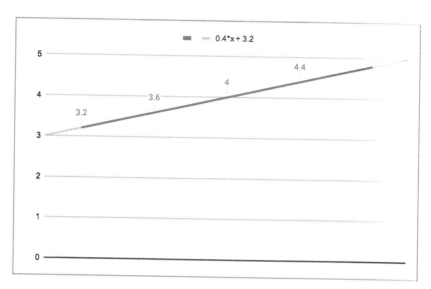

FIGURE 6.4 Trendline for Four Data Points.

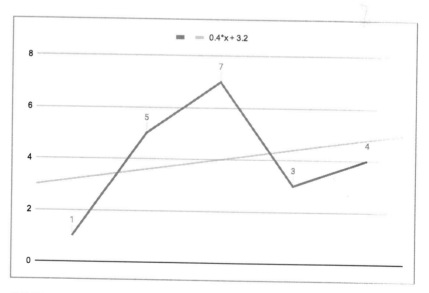

FIGURE 6.5 Trendline for Four Data Points.

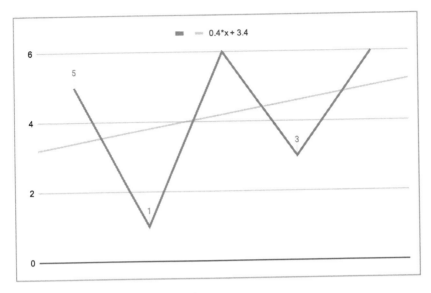

FIGURE 6.6 Trendline for Four Data Points.

by what is happening in their bodies, their minds, their families, their communities, and their worlds.

What is a Learning Curve?

The learning curve is an example of how even multi-dimensional data can be misrepresented without context. Learning to play violin is often described as having a steep learning curve. When people say this, generally they mean that if you graphed the playing abilities of a developing violinist on a graph, it would look something like Figure 6.7.

Parents of young violin players would say that parents' enjoyment of their students' practicing probably also follows a similar curve with the y-axis endpoints of "would poking my eardrums out be less painful" to "sobbing uncontrollably at the genius and beauty of my child's playing." There is a misleading lack of context in this chart. Similar to how you might drive up a hill zig-zagging side to side, a learning curve seems to suggest that there is little forward motion when the actual progress is greater and more complicated.

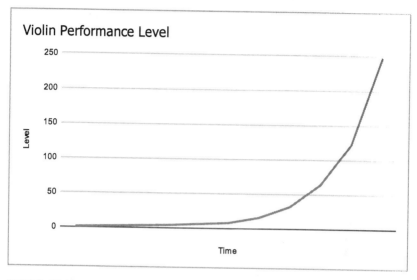

FIGURE 6.7 Playing Abilities of a Developing Violinist Over Time.

This is how it works in violin pedagogy. When I was studying at the Ohio State University, I took a year of classes with Dr. Robert Gillespie. He is considered by many one of the leading string pedagogy experts in the country. One of the maxims that came out of his class is "bows for Christmas." This meant that when students start learning violin in the fall, he did not have them play with the bow until around December. If playing with the bow was charted on a graph, it would display the steep learning curve I was just talking about. However, it is more accurate to think about driving up a mountain by zig-zagging across it.

While students were not playing with the bow until Christmas, Dr. Gillespie's approach was that students would be doing all kinds of pre-bow exercises – holding a pencil, telling stories with the bow, having finger exercise challenges on the bow, bowing in a paper towel tube. All of this meant that when the student finally put the bow to the violin, the sound would be beautiful and self-affirming rather than the stereotypical screeching sound of violin beginners. If experiences with the bow and pre-bow exercises were charted, it would follow a more linear shape, even though that shape is not reflected in the actual violin playing.

Sometimes when we don't see growth, it is not that there is no growth going on, it is possible that the growth is just happening in a different dimension. When evaluating mountain climbers, the more context available allows us to accurately see where climbers are at and give them useful, timely direction on how to continue to move forward. By definition, any kind of standardized test can only offer a one-dimensional snapshot of a certain type of learning at a certain time. Being able to use a variety of assessments, including lots of day-to-day personal interactions with the student, results in a more actionable measure of how to advance student learning.

Data Leading to Action

This does not mean that this kind of one-dimensional data is never relevant or important. There has been and will continue to be calls for the suspension or eradication of standardized tests after the pandemic because of the lack of context. Even in these unprecedented times, data with no context can be more useful than no data at all.

In areas that experience flash flooding, a raw altitude measurement can be very important. It can mean the difference between life or death. Knowing the altitudes of various community members would allow first responders to prioritize their responses – do we send the helicopter, do we have time for a boat, who do we need to attend to first? There is a debate on whether standardized tests that students take actually offer this level of accuracy, but accepting the premise that the tests do what they say they do, appropriately responding to this raw data could vastly alter students' lives. There are levels of raw data that should alarm us and move us toward highly intensive and effective interventions no matter what the cost. Generally, the greater the need, the less the context matters. When a flood victim is at the risk of drowning, it does not matter much how they got there, emergency measures are needed.

Just like flash flooding, the relevance of this one-dimensional data is very location-specific. It is not surprising that affluent, opportunity-rich communities have generally been leading the charge to suspend the standardized testing. These families have a myriad of resources to support their children if they are drowning in low performances or learning challenges. Where resources are scarcer, the data, when it can be trusted and reliable, is an invaluable tool in applying emergency measures to keep students from drowning. When emergency measures are not needed, more context can allow teachers to create sustainable plans for moving all students to higher levels of learning.

Earlier in this chapter, I talked about my apparent stagnation in my reading growth in first grade. As noted, while my mother had ideas about different influences on this growth, she was also applying interventions. Our home had always been a "literacy-rich" environment filled with books and resources. She continued to show me books and started me on a progressive reading curriculum that I could work on at my own pace. If there was any connection to teeth development or anything else, she was doing everything she could to overcome those obstacles and make sure that in the dimensions that she could influence, she was doing everything possible to advance growth. It all seemed to work. By third grade I had caught up with my peers and I was even starting to excel. Through my classmates' teasing, I earned a nickname I was secretly proud of: the leader of the "nerd herd."

Teaching Parents and Students

I expressed many of the concepts from this chapter in a TedX talk I gave in 2018, "Organic Time: A Non-Linear Perspective on Student Growth." As I shared the talk at the live event and on social media later, I had a lot of parents share with me their stories of their children's uneven, unpredictable growth. I was honored that one parent even sent me a scan of his child's specific test scores showing assessments that went significantly above and below the trend line through the year.

Once parents have seen their child "make it," they breathe a sigh of relief and it is easy to talk about how a few low test scores don't define their child. In the midst of these low scores, it is harder. So teachers with their seven hours a day, five days a week front row seat to the variability of these students have an important job to educate parents on the myth of linear progress and the other lack of context in standardized testing. This is not so that parents will ignore the data, but that the data can become part of a large, complete picture of their child's learning and what the next steps for growth will be.

The teacher needs to inform their student mountain climber (and the climber's parents) that when progress is stilted, there may be some boulder, some block that is not immediately being detected. Teachers have years of experience moving around these rocks, clearing the boulders, and shoveling out debris. When an intervention is applied and it does not achieve the desired result, this is not the fault of the climber, it is just time to re-evaluate what might be in the way and how to get around it.

Teachers that continue to teach in this environment of high-stakes testing and data-driven accountability survive because they are given the freedom to create an environment where these tests and data are part of the broadest picture of who a student is and how the learning community can work together for continued growth.

How Do I Use This Tomorrow?

1. In what areas of life do you see the myth of linear growth? Are there any areas in which growth would be expected to be constant and regular? How could you send messages to your students about the normalcy of "bad days" and the non-linear patterns that growth takes?

2. What testing and data have you found useful in evaluating student learning and progress? What are you doing or could you do to ensure this data is communicated to students and parents in the broadest context possible?

3. How can you communicate to your students the balance between the usefulness of standardized testing and its limits? How can you communicate this to parents?

How Do We Learn This Together?

#OrganicTime. How have you seen students grow in less linear and more organic ways?

Putting standardized testing into the right context is easier when you have a team of educators to collaborate with and connect with. Establishing and maintaining these relationships are covered in Chapter 7.

7

Don't Do This Alone

"Hold up, I got Bill Manchester on the line…" The excitement was palpable as I joined the conference call. All of the voices on the line fell silent as they listened for my informed response. What exciting knowledge bomb was I about to drop on this conversation?

> The note in question does not appear on any fingering charts because of an archaic way of writing that transposed horn parts down an octave when written in the bass clef. Just read it as if it were an octave higher.

This was not exactly edge-of-your-seat content. The excitement did not come from the answer, but from the process of collaboration. We were working together again, even if just for a few minutes.

Leading this call was Patrick Murphy, the Director of Bands at Maysville Local Schools in eastern Ohio. Just out of college, I was hired to teach general music and be the assistant band director with Patrick. For two years we had a highly collaborative, joyful working relationship. At times it looked like tag team wrestling. Patrick would be on the podium working the students through the rhythmic intricacies of a piece when all of the sudden I tagged in to tune the V7 chord with the altered ninth, then

DOI: 10.4324/9781003251330-8

back to Patrick to refine the contour of the phrasing in the wood-winds. I step in to offer an alternate trombone slide sequence; Patrick is back up to refine the suspended cymbal technique. And on and on.

How a Great Mentor Kept Me Teaching

The excitement that comes from a colleague that you work well together with is a gift that keeps a teacher teaching. From wearing matching fish ties to picking out inspirational movie clips to jamming out with the fifth-grade band on electric guitar and bass, my years working alongside Patrick were a joyful time of great student learning.

When I left Maysville to pursue my graduate degree and other teaching positions, Patrick remained a valuable colleague and mentor. While I was happy to help him out with the horn transposition question, his advice to me over the years has been far more poignant.

Later in my career, I was the assistant band director and de facto percussion instructor at another school. The head director and I had noticed that the high school percussionists were not being very careful about how they were using mallets, drum sticks, and other percussion equipment. This can be a financial concern if instruments and equipment are damaged, but it is also true that one aspect of being a musician in an ensemble is taking responsibility for equipment, particularly when it is shared across different ensembles.

Our solution was to require these high school percussionists to purchase their own mallets and drum sticks. We worked with a local music company to put together an affordable collection of appropriate, professional-grade mallets and sticks for around $80.

(For anyone not familiar with instrumental ensemble teaching in the United States, most students in instrumental ensembles (bands, orchestras) are required to purchase their own individual instruments for hundreds, if not thousands of dollars. The maintenance and care of these instruments is also up to the individual student, which can easily mean up to $80 per year. There is a valid, ongoing discussion on whether this is a good/appropriate model for music education in the United States, but this is the model that the students were used to. Financial assistance was available for students, but most parents in the district were very comfortable making those financial investments for their students' music education.)

A few days after this policy was introduced, a leader in the percussion section announced that he was going to take care of mallets for everyone in the section. He was not going to order them through the music company we had been working with, but he "had it all taken care of." The deadline arrived for the percussion section to have their own mallets and the leader arrived with mallets he had crafted himself. There were a dozen or so dowel rods topped with ping pong balls and rubber bouncy balls.

This was not what we had in mind when we asked for the students to provide their own mallets. The student's mallets were not able to produce a loud or stable tone quality and there were concerns that they might cause damage to the instruments. I told the student that these mallets would not be acceptable. He and the other percussionists would need to purchase the mallet collection we had assembled or other professionally produced mallets and sticks.

This was not acceptable to him or his mom. After a series of conversations with the student, his mom, and the assistant principal, we reached an impasse. The assistant principal supported our position that asking for professionally produced mallets was a legitimate request, but the student's mom did not. The mom made it clear that it was not a financial issue, but an academic one. Her son had creatively gone above and beyond for his classmates and he should be rewarded, not punished, for that ingenuity.

The root problem in this situation was that I had not established a trusting relationship with the percussion students at large and that student in particular. For a variety of reasons, the relationship had been very combative. The student's ingenuity just looked to me like he was trying to manipulate a situation so that he and the other percussionists did not have to do what we asked.

Frustrated, I called Patrick, who had been a percussion major at one of the premiere music conservatories in the US. I said, how could this kid really think that he could make mallets as good as professionals can? Patrick responded that actually mallets are not that hard to make and you can save a lot of money making them yourself if you have the right materials. He said, I know a guy who used to do this. Let me send you his information.

I wrote an e-mail humbly apologizing to the student and his mom and explaining the new plan. There would be an extension on having mallets for the section; if the student was willing to purchase the higher-quality materials, he could make mallets for the section. The total cost for replicating the $80 mallet package was now under $15. In a few days, he was excited to show me and the rest of the percussion section his new mallets. The mallets had a great tone and they lasted a long time.

This advice did not completely change the tenor of my relationship with the percussion student, but it did move the relationship in a positive direction. It kept me from souring a relationship with a band parent/community member and it was also just much better teaching than the direction I had been set on. Due to Patrick's advice, we solved our original problem of needing percussion students to feel ownership of their materials. Above and beyond that, the student and I learned about sound production, materials, and engineering.

This was not the only time that Patrick calmed me down and redirected me pedagogically, personally, or professionally. Several times in my career, I felt discouraged and not sure I could go on. The advice Patrick gave me not only made me feel better, but it often reset my thinking making the learning richer for students and more rewarding for me as a teacher. Having mentors and friends like Patrick is a big reason why teachers don't quit.

Finding Your Giraffe Friends

In the introduction to this book, when I told students the Fable of the Fox and the Grapes and asked them what the fox should do next, every class had the idea that the fox could ask other animals to help him. In a reality where foxes have metacognition, it seemed natural that there would be other animals that would communicate with the fox and that these animals with their unique resources would be available to help. It was a given that the fox would have some giraffe friends that would help him out.

While I was very fortunate with Patrick to connect deeply very early on in our working relationship, sometimes those giraffe friends for teachers seem not as given. But they are out there. Even just the realization that there are others that care about the successful learning of your students like you do can make a huge difference. There are parents, administrators, community members, and other teachers who also care a lot about these students. These stakeholders are often very ready and willing to invest time, energy, expertise, and finances to come alongside teachers they see investing in their students.

This was seen in some of the most unsung heroes of the emergency pandemic online teaching moment – the distance learning adjuncts. There were millions of parents, grandparents, babysitters, older siblings, and neighbors that suddenly became a child's tech assistant and distance learning adjunct. When these stakeholders saw teachers making this crazy pandemic online distance learning work, many of them stepped up to help in whatever way they could.

Thank you to the unidentified cameraperson running through the house as their child is virtually chased in our fox game. Thank you to the dad popping into the frame to ask for the guitar chords to our intro song so that he can play along next time. Thank you to the mom doing the cha-cha along with her third grader. Thank you to the rec center teacher who helped his students upload dozens of FlipGrid videos one rainy afternoon. Thank you to the babysitters who sang along on the partner song videos. Thank you to the dad who heard his daughter recording "What A Wonderful World" and decided he should be a part of the recording as well. Thank you, giraffe friends. We would not have been able to get through that crazy time without you.

When everyone's world was upside down, and even in the midst of the mood swings of the American public from teachers are-our-heroes to get-the-lazy-teachers-back-in-school, there were parents, grandparents, random neighbors, and others ready to help teachers succeed. If there were giraffe friends ready to help in those very unideal circumstances, I think giraffe friends can be counted on at any time.

Taking Competition Out of Teaching

While there are teaching relationships that are almost instantly collaborative, positive, and productive, other teaching relationships seem automatically combative, negative, and draining. Instead of a job characterized by joyful cooperation, teaching days become characterized by suspicious, distrustful competition. Whose students are learning the most and the fastest? Which class is out of control? Who has the best relationships with their students? Which teachers do the parents compliment the most? Who has won the most awards? Who gets the most recognition from the administration?

When teachers are not working together, it is easy for jealousy to take hold. Teachers will often not be treated the same and there is an appropriate push toward reaching for equality. But this is done the best when everyone feels like they are working together. That means that if someone is not being treated the same as me, it affects me and my teaching because we are connected. If you feel like another teacher is getting better treatment than you, one strategy is to connect your teaching to that teacher in a way that causes your mistreatment to affect their teaching.

Jealousy can often lead to gossip, with teachers minimizing the efforts and successes of others. These are sentiments I have heard from teachers:

- ◆ Yeah, his marching band always get the best ratings in the state, but I hear they start practicing all of the music in the spring instead of focusing on their concert music.
- ◆ Yeah, she's winning awards for her students' creative writing, but does that actually translate into marketable skills?
- ◆ Sure his students do well on the AP tests. If I had students that were so into their subjects, my students would ace the AP tests also.

There is place for collaborative discussions on how students can excel in all dimensions, but these only make sense when talking to the teacher in question, not while postulating to minimize other teachers' successes.

Seeing different teachers approach great teaching and learning can be like seeing different travelers approaching the same city from different directions.

Istanbul has been at the crossroads of trans-continental transportation for a very long time. To an extent like almost no other place in the world, travelers can be far away from each other in very different places experiencing very different things, but still be headed toward Istanbul.

A German traveler sitting in the Frankfurt airport is experiencing very different sights, smells, sounds, climate, and culture than an Ethiopian traveler sitting in the Addis Ababa airport. If someone didn't know much about air travel or geography, it might be hard to imagine that they could be sitting next to each other drinking coffees at the Starbucks in the Istanbul airport in a matter of hours.

This is like teaching. When we see a teacher teaching a certain way, it may be hard to believe we are all are trying to get our students to the same pedagogical place. However, once we get there we realize that the destination can be approached from many different directions. Even though we are starting in different places, we can still reach the same destination.

This analogy breaks down a bit as great teaching and learning is not a final destination that we live in, but rather a new journey we make every time we start interacting with our students. Some days we start in Greece and barely make it across the border. Other days we start in Kyrgyzstan and are able to catch that direct flight to Istanbul.

We often think of our own teaching in terms of our best days – those days when we came the closest to reaching our ideal of great teaching and learning, the days we made it to Istanbul. When we compare those best days with the best days of our colleagues, we see that we are much closer to each other than we might have originally thought.

Blessing Others

In my faith tradition, there is an instruction to "bless those that cause you harm." Once when I was reflecting on this instruction, tense conversations that I had had with a teaching colleague came to mind. Perhaps I shouldn't have, but I felt harmed by what my colleague had said. I felt disrespected and shut down. The conversation felt like a competition and I had lost. In my reflection time, I began to think about what blessing this person would look like. I realized I had found myself doing the opposite of blessing this person. I was secretly (and maybe not so secretly) hoping that the teaching ideas that they insisted were superior to mine would fail. I wanted harm to come on this person's teaching. This can be called the opposite of blessing, cursing.

I started to change my thinking. Whenever I saw or heard about things this person was doing, I meditated on things going well for them. Even if I would have done it a different way, I forced myself to hope that it goes well and that the students experience the kind of joyful, deep learning that we want for our students at all times. As I adopted this practice, my relationship with this colleague changed. I was rooting for everything they were doing. I began to genuinely feel good about their successes, even though I would have done it differently. Suddenly, I found myself wanting to copy things this colleague was doing. They were starting to have some really great ideas! It seemed as if they understood my philosophy. What really happened is that I started to understand theirs.

I expanded this practice so that whenever I saw something great that another teacher was doing or if I heard parents, administrators, or community members mention something great about another teacher, I would enthusiastically pass it on to that teacher, regardless of any philosophical differences I might have with their teaching style. It's hard to feel like you are competing with someone when you are talking about how great they are.

This practice of magnifying the greatness of others is a quality that I have observed in many great teachers. Molly Davis, for instance, was a fifth-grade teacher at Cassingham Elementary in Bexley City Schools. She was the kind of teacher that every parent wanted their kid to have. In 1984, she was recognized as the Ohio Teacher of the Year. One of her signature practices was having students create time capsules that they could come back and open with her when they were in high school.

Toward the end of her career, I was directing an elementary choir in a festival held at her school. She sent me a beautiful, detailed e-mail noting the ways that my co-director and I had engaged her students in the audience and thanking us for giving her students such a wonderful learning opportunity. I did not know that she was one of the best teachers in the state. I didn't know that her teaching practices were emulated across the district. I did know that she took the time to recognize the great teaching and learning that she saw going on, reminding me that we were all working together for all the students we come into contact with.

Astute readers will notice that I am speaking of Molly in the past tense. In 2011, in the midst of what was to be her last year of teaching before retirement, she died in a car accident. The school community was wrecked by this tragedy. In order to help students with the ongoing trauma of losing someone so dear so suddenly, the district established several ways of remembering Molly's legacy. A garden/outdoor learning space was built next to the school building; Each year elementary students observe Molly Davis Day, revisiting timeless aspects of her teaching philosophy.

For me, Molly's legacy will be the e-mail she sent to me. While I could have interacted with her through her amazing teaching practices or multiple awards, she was more interested in building me up and recognizing together what great teaching and learning we had shared.

Great colleagues can make the difference in whether teachers stay with teaching or quit. We can begin to have these kinds of relationships by being the kind of encouraging, uplifting colleague that we want to have and looking for and believing the best about those around us.

How Do I Use This Tomorrow?

1. What is the last positive thing you heard about a teacher in your building or district? Did you pass that on to the teacher? What great teaching and learning have you noticed in the past week that you could directly mention to one of your teaching colleagues?
2. Are there any teachers, administrators, staff, or faculty that you find it difficult to have a positive relationship with? Commit time imagining how they can be successful with their students in their role. Train your brain that whenever you think of this person, you have a positive image of them being successful in their role with the students.
3. If you have someone that you feel like you don't work well with because you have conflicting teaching philosophies or ideas, try to arrange for or ask them about a time when they felt like teaching was going great. Ask follow-up questions and see if your idea of great teaching and learning working are closer together than you may have first thought.

How Do We Learn This Together?

#DontTeachAlone. Who have been your biggest mentors and best colleagues in teaching? How have they supported you?

While relationships with other teachers are a big reason that teachers don't quit teaching, the relationships and growth in students is what most teachers find most rewarding about the job. This is celebrated in the next chapter.

8

The Power of Great Teaching and Learning

The woman was on my case the entire year… it wasn't my first rodeo of teaching. I had been teaching like three years. So I had years under my belt and you know, every time I turn around I was being called in by the principal and all this kind of stuff because this woman was all upset.

This is Kim Rhodes. At this time, she was a fifth-grade teacher in a suburban school district. The criticism Kim was receiving had nothing to do with what was actually happening in her classroom.

I always did a lot of hands-on activities with the kids… In 42 minutes, I wanted to be able to hit all of them one way or the other. So, when I taught history, yes, there will be lectures, but also, for instance the battle of Lexington and Concord; we talked about the Redcoats and how they marched through the night. So, I had all of the kids get out into the hallway and we were all stacked together three or four in a row. I taught them the goose step. They had to goosestep like a redcoat all around the building, down the stairs, synchronized and everything. Yeah, I remember one girl coming back and she said, "Oh my gosh, Ms. Rhodes, that's wonderful for a thigh workout!"

DOI: 10.4324/9781003251330-9

The evidence of great teaching and learning was apparent throughout Kim's teaching.

> Something that you might even want to do is when you have to test them on certain things, let them come in and have input on their project. You know, I'd have a series of questions to ask them, and if they could answer them right off the top of their heads and things like that, I would say marvelous! Now, what grade do you think? Or what percentage do you think you deserve? And they would tell me, and they always graded themselves low. And I would say, well, I disagree. And then they look and I would say I think instead of it being an 88 as you said, I think it's a 95. So, let's compromise.

Kim was allowing students to have ownership of their own learning in ways many of them had never experienced before.

> A lot of them said that they've never other than me had a teacher allow them to have input into their own work.

Kim was teaching not just what she knew, but also what she had experienced.

> The secret... was I taught not only from the book, but I taught from personal experience. Particularly as when we got into closer, serious issues after the foundation of the United States. I taught it from the view of a woman. So, it was a very well-rounded education.

And while Kim had strong confidence in her teaching, she was also humble enough to know she'd didn't always have all of the answers.

> And I had a professor who said, "Be honest, don't go in there and try to think that you are the master of everything because you're here. You don't know, and it's OK to tell kids, I don't know." Even my own subject that I taught for

30 years, American history, there were things I didn't know. When kids would ask... I would listen and go, "Wow, I don't know the answer to that. I will research that tonight and we'll discuss it tomorrow." I mean, it's okay and I think when sometimes I said that to the kids, they were startled.

Kim guided her students in hands-on interactive deep learning. Students were growing in the academic subjects that Kim taught, as well as growing as independent, strong thinkers. She modeled humility and intellectual curiosity to her students. This is not why she was being called to the principal's office.

There was a mother opening day, you know, in elementary how the teachers stand at the door and that kind of stuff and welcome the kids. This one woman walked up to me and said, "Oh no, my child will not have a black teacher."

The opposition to Kim teaching had nothing to do with her philosophical approach or actual teaching. Kim was a great teacher, but she found herself in a terrible teaching situation because of racist views of parents and an administration that would not confront these views.

Well finally her daughter left and went to the [next] grade. And I can remember that it must have been a week into the new school year. Principal called me in and said that the woman had gone to the Board of Education and launched a complaint that I wasn't qualified to teach in their schools any more... and the Superintendent was meeting and everything else. And I said, wait a minute, you all are meeting on me and my constitutional rights are being violated right now. Well, their eyes got big because they didn't realize that my uncle was the federal judge that made the disaggregation decision for Columbus Public Schools, Judge Duncan.

Robert Martin Duncan was the first African American to serve as a federal judge in Ohio. He decided the case that led to the desegregation of one of the largest school districts in the state, Columbus City Schools. In addition to ruling on the case, Robert Duncan also directly oversaw the implementation of the desegregation plan.

I went into the nurse's office because of course this was in 79–80 when there was no cell phone. So, I went and got on the nurse's phone because she wasn't there that day and I called my dad. Dad called Uncle Bobby off the bench. Uncle Bobby took the call and said you tell them right now you're giving them 48 hours to solve this issue, or you're taking it to channel four, six, and ten and you are going to blow [the district] out of the water and tell them that this is advice from your counsel. And I walked right back into [the principal's] office and I told him word for word what my uncle Bob had said. And honest to God within 24 hours I had a letter that said the issue was dead.

The legal battle had been won, but that did not change the fact that there were parents and others in the district who were judging Kim, not by the quality of her teaching, but by the color of her skin. There was still a morale battle that Kim would have to deal with.

So I turned around. By then I was saying I'm done with this district. I am done. This is ridiculous.

Somehow Kim continued and not just continued, but thrived. The ideological change in the school community did not come from a legal decision, but from the power of great teaching and learning. Parents saw how their students were able to grow, and soon the script was flipped. Parents were begging to have Kim teach their children.

I'll never forget my last day before I retired and stepped out of Jones, there was a mother that walked up and said you've had three of my four children. Could you stay one more year so my last child could have you?

There is tremendous power in great teaching and learning. In Kim's case, it was the power to educate and change a community. For many teachers, the power of great teaching and learning is what keeps them teaching, even when they feel like quitting.

(The preceding paragraphs are excerpts from the podcast, A Different EduPodcast. *#DidntQuitTeaching: Kim Rhodes* was initially released January 2021. Available at Apple podcasts and other major podcast distributors.)

The Power of Great Teaching and Learning

From Betsy Seipel, an elementary teacher Waynesfield-Goshen Local Schools:

I… think back to my first year teaching 4th grade and having a kid that was known as being the problem kid and he told me that he was always the kid who got in trouble. I had a conversation with him one day and said I didn't know him in the past, only now and that I knew he had the ability to do well in school. He turned a corner that year and wanted to do his best. On the last day of school, he was the last to leave my room and he came to me with tears in his eyes and told me he didn't want to leave because it was the best year ever, which brought me to tears. When I have a bad day, I always remind myself of that to keep me going.

From an anonymous teacher on aDifferentEduSite.com:

I continued teaching because former students that I stayed in touch with reminded me of how much I did for them.

It is very affirming when students and parents communicate directly about the effect that a teacher has had on their learning. Many teachers who have kept teaching even when they felt like quitting have a story (or several) about specific times students and parents communicated to them about their learning. For many teachers, knowing the impact they are having is why they continue to teach.

Celebrating the Signs of Great Teaching and Learning

There are also subtler, less direct ways that teachers can see the signs of great teaching and learning. There are times that learning flows in a way that feels less directly connected to the teacher. In these instances, students are not as likely to communicate a teacher's influence directly. I think it is like someone learning to speak a second language. The greatest compliment someone speaking a second language can receive is no compliment at all. The speaking is so natural that the native speakers don't even realize the person is speaking a second language. Even when a teacher does not receive a direct message about the effect of their teaching, there are signs that can be celebrated to acknowledge that the teaching objective has definitely been achieved.

I was walking out of the school after a long evening of multiple performances. We had just completed our annual arts fest. Student artwork had been mounted on every available inch of wall space at the school and my co-teacher and I had organized multiple singing, acting, and instrumental performances, complete with professional rock musicians. A father that had five kids in my performances that night turned around with the most genuine smile and said, "thanks for making music class not lame." This is very different than Betsy's story about the student letting her know how she changed his life. But for me it was a very positive sign that students were learning and experiencing something great. I'm not the only person this resonated with. Years later, I related this story to a principal I met on a flight. He arranged for me to interview at his school a few days later. Objective achieved.

When my daughter was in middle school her orchestra directors invited a professional string trio in for a one-day residency and concert. The students learned new music quickly, improvised with the professionals, and worked on their stage presence for the concert. I don't think my daughter said anything to her directors about the day, but she told me that she was now a "real musician" after working with the professionals. Objective achieved.

Chad Stearns was the band director when my sister was in high school at Waynesfield-Goshen Local Schools. When Chad took over the instrumental music program, there was a very wide range of skills and experience among a very small number of band students. In addition to creatively arranging and selecting music that differentiated for these levels, Chad also leveraged his professional connections to offer students performing opportunities outside of his program. He was teaching motivated, talented students like my sister that he trusted them to represent him outside of the school. The talented, motivated players rose to the occasion time and time again. Objective achieved.

For many years Bexley Middle School social studies teachers Mindy Hall and Beth Jax led their students through an immersive study into the history and current political climate of the country of South Sudan. Students learned directly from recent immigrants from South Sudan as well as raising funds for a native-led organization providing resources to the South Sudanese people. While students probably let Mindy and Beth know how much the unit meant to them, the more profound signs of teaching and learning were the dramatic responses of the students. One student donated the money she had received from her bat mitzvah to the organization. Another student's parents purchased advertising on a billboard to help raise funds. Students utilized their art and musical skills to produce designs, videos, and posters to raise awareness. Objective achieved.

Not Missing Moments of Great Teaching

Teachers renew themselves through the power of great teaching and learning, not only by creating great teaching and learning opportunities themselves but also by collaborating with students to create and define their own great teaching and learning moments.

It was the last day of school and during the slide show at the annual fifth grade rising up ceremony, my mind was wandering to the tasks that I needed to take care of before checking out for the summer break. David Schottner, a fifth-grade teacher-colleague, was squeezing out the last possible moments of great teaching and learning.

As the slide show played, he watched carefully with the student tech assistant operating the laptop. David had picked up on the students' nervousness about everything going right. Rather than brushing it off or telling the student that mistakes would not be a big deal, David entered right into the moment. "Okay, here's the song transition. Oh, it should be starting. Come on, oh, here it goes. Phew! We got it. Here's the next one..." And on he went with the student through the full ten-minute slide show. David knew that the slide show was a big deal to the student and so it was a big deal to David.

It would have been perfectly acceptable for David to sit silently watching the slide show go by, admiring the students' work from a distance, but instead he figuratively and literally sat beside the student, creating and defining a moment of great teaching and learning.

Great Teaching and Learning Keeps Teachers Going

Hopefully the preceding chapters gave you some tools to be able to overcome some of the challenges in your current teaching situation. Over time, however, some of these challenges will return. If great teaching and learning is not happening, any challenge can feel like enough of a reason to quit. Conversely, when things are going well, master teachers become master learners, capable of innovating and inventing their way into great teaching and learning despite challenging circumstances.

How Do I Use This Tomorrow?

1. Make a list of your top five teaching moments in the last two years. Spend some time thinking about these if they don't come quickly. Write them down or post them in a place where you can revisit them. Update this list every semester. Not only is this a good list to refer to when thinking about overcoming obstacles, but writing these moments down will make it easier to identify them as they happen.

2. Each discipline tends to have its own indirect ways that students show their learning. What indirect ways have you seen students displaying their learning? Ask other teaching colleagues in your discipline what they have

seen and then think of ways to look for these signs in the students you currently teach and in students that have moved beyond your classroom.

How Do We Learn This Together?

#PowerOfLearning. How have you seen learning change lives and communities?

Even when great teaching and learning are going on, sometimes it is still not enough to overcome the feelings of quitting teaching. There are many reasons teachers feel like quitting and some of these cannot be overcome by the energy, optimism, and motivation of an individual teacher. The last chapter examines what happens then.

Conclusion

When You Feel Like Quitting Teaching, It's Okay If You Do

When I was working on this book, I talked to a lot of teachers and former teachers. When I said the phrase "quit teaching," all of them had a strong reaction. Teachers who retired felt like in different circumstances, maybe they could have gone longer. Teachers who quit young often held a bitterness toward an education system that had deep faults preventing it from living up to its audacious promises. All of these former teachers wanted to explain and offer a sort of apology that they did not do more and go farther for their students.

The main message of this book is that if you feel like quitting teaching, you might be able to find the tools and inspiration needed to be able to keep going. Lots of teachers have faced many different obstacles that made them feel like quitting. Many of these teachers found ways to overcome these obstacles, not just getting by, but returning to the great teaching and learning that they fell in love with in order to enter the profession.

A corollary of this message is if you feel like quitting it's okay if you quit. All teachers stop teaching at some point. There are lots of teaching situations that cannot be solved by the chapters in this book or any book.

There are over three million teachers in the United States. So, there are over three million unique work-life combinations

DOI: 10.4324/9781003251330-10

that US teachers are experiencing. These run the gamut from "should-be/probably-are-illegal" to "I-can't-believe-someone-is-paying-me-to-have-fun-like-this."

There are teachers in situations like the one that Kim Rhodes faced that do not have the connections and stamina to be able to mount an appropriate legal battle for their rights. For some of these teachers, there is no option other than quitting.

And at the same time, sometimes in the same city or county, there are teachers experiencing community, beautiful learning, support, and all the things we were promised about teaching. Even though some days are better than others for these teachers, they feel rewarded personally, professionally, and financially to a degree that makes continuing teaching highly favorable to quitting.

There are millions in between these two extremes trying to figure out whether they can stay and push on or they are in the cohort that needs to get out. Because of the emotional/passion/calling component of teaching, this decision becomes very intense for many teachers.

The polarity of our current cultural climate has not made things easier. There has been enormous pressure put on teachers to stick it out and not give up on these kids. This has been followed by pushback to that pressure that caused any encouragement to teachers to persevere to be seen as gaslighting and ignoring the realities of teaching. It is very possible that critics will find material in this very book to be overly simplistic and non-empathetic to the true problems teachers are facing.

This heightens the emotional load on teachers trying to make tough decisions about their careers. Is there something wrong with me if I am not willing to make some sacrifices to be able to help students learn? If I am not willing to give 110% all of the time am I doing the students a disservice to keep teaching? If I don't teach these students, who will? If I don't stand up for my emotional health and well-being and the emotional health and well-being of other teachers, who will?

Not only are there three million different work–life situations that teachers are in, but there are also three million different types of teachers living in these situations. As teachers navigate this space between quitting and continuing forward, the decision becomes clearer if it is not clouded by voices assuming that what they would do or not do is the right decision for another teacher.

Teachers need to protect each other from abuse and discrimination and young teachers can gain wisdom from veteran teachers' perspectives about the long-term ramifications of a skewed work–life balance, but teachers need to not assume that another teacher is just like them and will experience a teaching situation the same way. It is hard to overestimate how different one person is from another person. When it comes to teaching situations, there are circumstances that one teacher finds acceptable and able to excel in and another teacher finds completely unmanageable.

If You Quit Teaching

For teachers who decide to quit teaching, particularly earlier than originally planned or related to these present difficulties, it might be difficult to imagine you (or anyone else) feeling good about the decision you made.

I was trading shifts with my wife while my 9-month-old daughter was in the ICU after spinal surgery. I can't remember if the nurse saw the book I was reading or the lesson plans on my iPad or it came up in conversation, but somehow she figured out that I was a teacher.

"I used to be a teacher," the nurse replied pleasantly. She told me she had taught in the large city district where the hospital was located. The nurse was much younger than me, so it seemed fairly apparent that she had not taught for long.

I thought the conversation was moving on, but, like so many others, she wanted to explain.

"It wasn't the kids, you know," she randomly volunteered. "The kids were great. I loved all the kids."

The nurse continued talking about her disappointment with the realities of teaching all the while expertly checking the vitals for my daughter, adjusting the IV machines, giving my daughter a high quality of care. My daughter had a tethered cord; a piece of fatty tissue had caused the spinal cord to not be able to move below a certain portion of her spine. The doctors cut open her back and sliced this connection. My infant daughter had to lay very still for several days, appropriately sedated, so her spine would heal properly. My daughter's medical team, including this ICU nurse, held my daughter's life in their hands. Not properly attending to the healing could mean loss of bodily functions, paralysis, and even death.

In those middle-of-the-night moments when she was so expertly caring for my daughter in ways that I couldn't, I was very glad that this former teacher had become a nurse.

For teachers who feel like they would be letting students, parents, or communities down, there are many important roles that people hold in a community. Any disappointment that you or those around you may feel about the decision to quit teaching might be quickly overridden by the opportunities that you are able to find later.

Life Satisfaction Does Not Have to Come From a Job

Conversely, for both teachers that quit teaching and teachers that continue, it is important to realize that life satisfaction does not have to come from a job. Teachers feel an intense calling to the profession and to their students. When I talk to my non-teaching friends about their jobs, few, if any other professions illicit this kind of response.

I remember eating breakfast with a friend and I asked him a question about how fulfilling a certain task for his job was. He just laughed and said, "Oh, no, my job doesn't work that way." This friend of mine is one of the most thoughtful, profound people I know. He works in healthcare. He doesn't work directly with patients, but he could easily make the connection between what he does and how it positively affects the health of patients if he was looking for satisfaction through his job.

He's not. He finds satisfaction in providing a steady, reliable income to take care of his family. He finds satisfaction in having time and energy to pursue other interests and passions.

Although many teachers look for the personal satisfaction/ fulfilling rewards of teaching because the profession does not offer the level of financial rewards that other professions do, it's okay if it is not always fulfilling. We are human beings and our enthusiasm, interests, and joy will modulate based on many factors that are outside of our classroom. Changes in the degree of enthusiasm, motivation, and joy in teaching should be expected. This doesn't necessarily mean that you need to leave teaching. It could mean settling in to a different rhythm, a different mode of enthusiasm, motivation, and joy that includes other priorities outside of teaching.

For Teachers Who Persist

For teachers who plan to continue teaching despite their less than positive feelings about the entirety of their situation, it is worth reiterating that solving any problems is only the means to the end of great teaching and learning. This great teaching and learning is what makes teachers want to keep teaching and be able to sustain long, fulfilling careers.

As Linette Morris, an elementary teacher at Northridge Local Schools wrote on her personal Facebook page:

> It's been a really busy week… Busy school year, actually. On top of being overwhelmed with a lot, I've been having behavior issues in my class lately. This afternoon the kids showed me (what I already knew, but enjoyed the reminder). That they have kind hearts. A shy struggling student raised her hand to share an answer, but then didn't want to finish the answer. One kid shouts out, "It's ok. You've got this!" Then kids started chiming in, "You can do it! You're so smart! I believe in you!"
> Made my day!!

If you are looking to teach for the long term, waiting for problems to be solved in order to get to great teaching and learning will leave you waiting most, if not all, of your career. Instead, as great teaching and learning is happening in the midst of less than ideal circumstances, use that energy and motivation to push for change, both in personal teaching practices and in larger structural policies and procedures.

The Days of Small Beginnings

For the teachers ready to apply their creativity, ingenuity, and optimism to making their teaching situation better, congratulations. I believe that even if you end up quitting, you will feel the best possible way about quitting if you have done whatever is in your power to make it work. And also, a final word of caution.

When teachers feel like quitting teaching, it is sometimes easy to think that a massive change in position, philosophy, approach, or location will make the difference. For some teachers these changes do make a big difference. But because no position, philosophy, or approach is perfect, teachers may find themselves soon needing another gigantic shift to feel like teaching again. It is easy to run out of these enormous shifts to make. A new position or a new approach can be a fresh catalyst to start change in a positive direction, but generally lasting change will be slow.

In the Jewish and Christian faiths, there is a prophet Zechariah. He asks, "who has despised the day of small things, of small beginnings?" I raise my hand sheepishly. I like big beginnings, massive revolutions, unbelievable growth patterns. I not only want to be the change in the world, I want to be it right now in a big way.

The prophet continues, "the Seven [a reference to the Divine] rejoice when they see the plumb line [the earliest steps of a construction process]." The context of this questioning and answering is a group of people that felt like quitting. It is describing a time that the Jewish people were rebuilding the main temple in Jerusalem, their capital city, after decades of exile and foreign oppression. Due to various factors, the construction had been halted. There were questions about whether it would ever continue and ever finish. There was divine joy at just the start, the small beginning of returning to that inspired process to which they had committed.

I want to be filled with joy at small beginnings. I want to be happy about the kid that comes up and talks to me about her weekend, even though she couldn't hold it together in my class and held the whole class back and even though she might do the same thing tomorrow. I want to let myself be joyful about the other day when I was able to move a disengaged student into the center of the learning knowing that for that one success there were ten classes where I never was able to engage him. I want to find the divine joy in the quick giggle of a child who does a dance with his classmates and forgets for a short time all of the reasons she has to be sad.

As we all move forward into a new time of teaching that will be forever marked by the enormous difficulties of the past few years, let us not despise the day of small beginnings, but find and build on the joy of great teaching and learning.

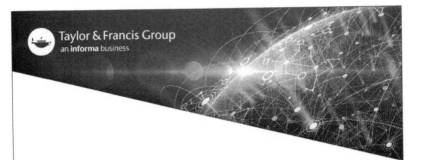